THE SECRET
LORE
OF THE CAT

THE SECRET LORE OF THE CAT

Fred Gettings

GRAFTON BOOKS

A Division of the Collins Publishing Group

LONDON GLASGOW
TORONTO SYDNEY AUCKLAND

Grafton Books
A Division of the Collins Publishing Group
8 Grafton Street, London W1X 3LA

Published by Grafton Books 1989

British Library Cataloguing in Publication Data

Gettings, Fred
The secret lore of the cat
1. Cats, Occult aspects
I. Title
133

ISBN 0-246-13468-2

Printed in Great Britain by
Butler and Tanner Ltd, Frome

Contents

Manx kittens; Fishing and Leopard Cats; jaguars and tigers; the Pallas Cat; Cat and Fiddle; the cat in heraldry.

The 'Stable cat'; the oracular cat; mistaken for lions of Judah; Corn cat lore; Freya's Day; the Book of Kells and the cross of Monasterboice; Iruscan, King of Cats; the Reverend Hawker's excommunicated cat; the Temple Mark; *Piers Plowman*; effigy of the Black Prince; de Honnecourt's cat; George Wither's Magistrate; Dick Whittington; 'The Owl and the Pussy Cat'; Puss in Boots again; the Cheshire Cat and the County Palatine; Ginger, the moggy in Narnia; another Aesop fairytale.

Cat and Man; the etheric cat; anthropomorphism; Darwinism and spiritual evolution; Tiger Swami and the inner cat; cats' healing power; ghostly and psychic cats; spirit photographs; demonic cats; warnings of disaster, presages of death; a de-bugged demonic cat?; the tiger tamed.

The cat as archetype; the sphere of the Moon; Purgatory; Lalande's constellation; the Chinese zodiac; the lion in alchemy; the Fool and the Juggler; the Kuykendall Tarot pack; the cats of Hieronymus Bosch; demonic music; an unrecognized treasure or the Devil in disguise?; Hogarth's dumb shows; the cat prostitute; cat among the pigeons; Henri Rousseau's cats.

Part II – The Hellish Cat

The anti-cat league and Pope Gregory IX; the feline Satan; Haborym, Flauros and Bael; St Peter's cat; the incubus; cat burning; Hans Baldung Grien; cat-demons of Japan, South America and the Scottish Hebrides.

Preface

I am the cat of cats. I am
    The everlasting cat!
Cunning, and old, and sleek as jam,
    The everlasting cat!
I hunt the vermin in the night –
    The everlasting cat!
For I see best without the light –
    The everlasting cat!

WILLIAM BRIGHTY RANDS

'Best without light' is 'the everlasting cat', sings William Rands in his finest poem. The cat thrives in the darkness for it is an occult creature, happier in the reflected light of the Moon than in the bright glare of the Sun's rays. The Sun in the skies is too steady for the everlasting cat, for her strange eyes are designed to fluctuate from full to slit, in imitation of that lesser luminary, the Moon. The cat is symbol of the night, of the lunar darkness and of the Moon's phases.

While the Sun has become a symbol of consciousness, of all that may be seen in the created world, the Moon has become a symbol of the unconscious. The ideal cat sits brooding over that deep well of hidden wisdom in every human soul. She made herself guardian of this secret pool of wisdom, and was at the very beginning of our recorded history worshipped as a god.

Besides being the symbol of inner wisdom, the Moon is a symbol of change, for in its monthly circuit of the earth it waxes and wanes to give those four distinctive stages we call the waxing crescent, the gibbous, the full and the waning crescent. For one short period each month it is like the crescent-shaped mouth of the Cheshire Cat in Carroll's story (figure

Fig. 1   The crescent smile of the bodyless Cheshire Cat, in Tenniel's illustration to Alice in Wonderland: the cards arguing about the beheading of a cat which has no body

Fig. 2 Goya's etching-aquatint 'Ensayos' (Trials). Goya used the cat familiar in the majority of his demonic and witchcraft images. His commentary on this picture, which shows a witch-novice, reads: 'Little by little, she is making progress'

1), the rest of the cat invisible to human eyes. Inevitably, the deified everlasting cat has taken into itself the implications of this changeable nature. The cat emerges throughout history as the representative of change, for her meaning in art and literature oscillates between two extremes: sometimes she is used as an image of nether Hell (figure 2), sometimes as a symbol of virginity (figure 9). She is at once a symbol of the everlasting purity, and a symbol of all that is temporary and fluctuating. Never, as Rands in his madness realized so well, is the cat represented as symbol of the pure solar light.

The everlasting cat found its way into my own heart in the darkness – significantly enough in the flickering half-light of a cinema. She started an interest in the occult lore of the cat in a way which I have never forgotten, even though I did not fully understand the experience at the time. In the film *Bell, Book and Candle*, Kim Novak played the part of a witch who owned a familiar cat called Pyewacket. This was the first intimation I had that the cat was a creature singled out for special attention by the occult realm, and in particular by the darker levels of witchcraft. I first saw this film about thirty years ago, and was enthralled by that short passage in which the slit-vision of the witch's cat is presented on the screen, and our familiar human vision was distorted by an elongating lens. I felt that there was something both powerful and familiar about that distortion – it was as though that elongated slit into space and time gave us a temporary vision which was somehow more real than real – one which we lesser mortals, with our quite ordinary rotund lens eyes, do not have. I had the sensation that this was how we ourselves saw the world before we were born.

It was only much later that I learned that this film cat had been called 'Pyewacket' after a famous witch familiar from occult history (see pages 177–8), and it was even later that I began to understand why that curious distortion of vision had moved me so deeply, and reminded me so strangely of birth. The cat's eyes –with what Keats called 'those bright languid segments green' – are more than lunar in shape. They are not exactly crescents, nor are they precisely the same shape as the gibbous moon. Even so, the shape was adopted by the ancient Egyptians as a symbol for birth ◊, an hieroglyphic which they called 'Ru'. This is the same symbol which the later occultists claim as the origin of the small circle on top of the magical symbol of the 'ankh' ♀ which is worn even in modern times as a protective amulet, but which figures in thousands of Egyptian sacred documents.

The original ankh speaks a secret language, for its graphic form represents a birth-passage from the spiritual world ◊ into the realm of space and time, represented by a sigil, the Tau cross T, which denotes extension in time and descent into matter. No wonder that the goddess Venus, who took to herself this ankh symbol in the form which is still used to represent the feminine principle ♀, should in mythology be transformed into a cat (see page 17). No wonder the cat should be linked in the mystery lore with birth, with the spiritual realms beyond the material world and with the strange mutations of the Moon.

The more I studied the occult lore, the more I became aware that in the symbolism of the cat there resided secrets which could only be expressed in terms of images and pictures, for when they were set out in words the inner power was lost. The two meanings for the word 'hermetic' are not accidental. The commonplace meaning is 'sealed in' or 'air-tight', and the second meaning, derived straight from the ancient mystery wisdom, is 'pertaining to Hermes'. Hermes is one of the enduring symbols of the Great Sage, the occult cosmic teacher who readily gives secret lore and wisdom to those who search with care and honesty.

For all his Greek name, Hermes was, like our own domestic cat, an ancient Egyptian, when his name was Thoth. The knowledge of Hermes – the later hermetic lore – was often said to be transmitted by pictures and symbols, for images could be 'sealed in' or made 'air-tight' (which is to say, impervious to the outer world). In comparison, words did not have the same sealed and hermetic quality – words were fragile things which lost their energies and changed their meanings, and were there-

Fig. 3   Sacred Egyptian Cat, the so-called 'Gayer-Anderson Cat', circa *30* B.C. *British Museum*

fore essentially unsuitable for transmitting knowledge of the secret things. As the modern poet T. S. Eliot (who, as we shall see, knew much about cats and their secret lore) wrote, 'words slip, slide and perish'. This is almost certainly the reason why the extraordinary bronze of the Egyptian cat-god (figure 3) says more about feline secrets than any words might do, and why almost any picture of a cat is more expressive of the mystery within the feline world than any number of words. Yet in modern times we have become impatient of real art, and have lost the faculty of quiet contemplation which the art of ancient times demands – we now expect even our images to leap up and down on silver screens. In modern times, even the symbols leak their secrets and discharge their energies, and so we must resort to words – even to words about images – if we wish to delve into the mystery of the cat.

If my interest in the strange duality of the everlasting and impermanent cat began in the lunar darkness of a cinema, this book was conceived as a result of my meeting with a magical cat. Two years ago I was commissioned to take some travel photographs of the mediaeval cities in Europe, and one early morning I found myself exploring the back streets of Ghent, seeking a suitable image to represent this lovely city. Belgium is a land of cat-lovers, and the Belgians, rather like the Dutch, love to have the colours of flowers stream into their rooms with the sunlight, and so I decided to try to photograph this characteristic.

I did not have far to go. No sooner had I turned into the back streets behind Lange Steenstrasse than a ginger tom appeared as though by

Fig. 4   Cat fighting Cock: illustration by Arthur Rackham to Aesop's fable of the Cat and the Cock. Drawn 1912

magic on the pavement, and leapt gracefully up to a nearby window, where he sat dutifully in the sunshine washing his sleek fur. The cat had chosen well, for alongside him were several terracotta pots which were singing a geranium redness into the morning air.

As I moved my camera towards this ideal scene the cat pertly lifted his nose, in the way of certain types of photogenic felines, and waited, as though knowing full well what I had in mind. I took the first of my pictures – a detail of his face – but then, to my surprise, a young woman appeared in my viewfinder: she was standing at the window, about to open it in order to let in her cat. The ginger sensed that breakfast was in the offing, and lightly brushed aside the photographic session to slide into the house. It was only then that the young woman saw me. She smiled, and signalled apology for having disturbed the cat. Was I photographing her flowers or the cat? she asked. Would I like some coffee? I nodded gratefully, and was soon standing by her easel drinking delicious Blue Mountain. She was an artist, and was working on the illustrations for a book on cats.

We talked for a while about cats and about drawings of cats. 'Do you know Rackham's cats?' she asked.

I nodded.

'In that case, you will certainly like this.' She went over to the window which I had recently been photographing, picked up a book and handed it to me. It was a book on the illustrator Arthur Rackham which I had written over a decade before, in which I had chosen to reproduce several of his cat pictures, from the tame household variety (figure 4) to the witchcraft familiars (figure 5).

What a magical cat her ginger tom had been to draw me with such cunning into his owner's house. That cat had not really been interested in having his photograph taken – he merely had access to the secret wisdom, and knew that his mistress and I should meet, talk about cats, Rackham and life. In later months, as I continued my long photographic project in Europe, I could not get the ginger out of my mind. I knew already that the cat is a magical creature, with an arcane symbolism special to itself, yet I had never before become personally entangled in the feline magic it can weave. Why was the cat so different from other animals? Why did even its appearance suggest that it is wreathed in mystery, and why do its eyes reveal it to be possessed of an altogether superior knowledge of the higher world? What was it about the cat which induced the Egyptians to build a whole world of symbolism

Fig. 5   Cat familiars flying ahead of the witches: illustration by Arthur Rackham to the 1907 edition of The Ingoldsby Legends: *'Hey! up the chimney, lass! Hey, after you!'*

around its eyes, its nature and its association with the Moon? And why were these ancient symbols so pregnant with meaning that they have endured for thousands of years, and are still found in many contemporary cultures? I am not sure that I know the answers to all these questions, yet for sure this book is the result of my attempt to set in some sort of order the various replies which the arcane tradition gives. It is in the arcane lore that we find attempts to explain how the everlasting cat, once deified and secure in the higher realm of the ideal world, eventually entered into the familiar realm of space and time, to appear in a thousand guises and a thousand different symbolic forms.

Introduction

But above and beyond there's still one name left over,
And that is the name you will never guess;
The name that no human research can discover –
But THE CAT HIMSELF KNOWS, and will never confess.

THOMAS STEARNS ELIOT
The Naming of Cats

There is a sense in which one need only look at a cat to see that it is a mysterious being. Of course, all created beings are mysterious and wrapped in mysteries, yet, somehow, the spiritual is more apparent or more transparent in the cat. One has the feeling that the cat is centred in itself – is at peace with itself and entirely its own thing. The great fifteenth-century occultist Cornelius Agrippa had as his personal Latin motto, 'Let no man who might belong to himself belong to another.' It is a perfect motto for an occultist, yet one which no cat would need, as the true feline takes it for granted that it should belong to no other than itself. The true cat is by virtue of its own inner disposition a natural occultist: outwardly, it is a creature of the night, a lunar goddess, yet inwardly it carries its own light, as though its consciousness were centred within itself. This inward-centring leads man to misunderstand the cat, for it is easy to mistake it for selfishness. In such a way one not conversant with the teachings of the Buddha may misunderstand the equanimity of the Buddhist, and assume an indifference in him to the sufferings in the world. There is a story that the cat was one of two animals who did not weep at the death of the Buddha, and this tale is told to the detriment of the cat – yet if one remembers that the cat has an inner wisdom, and carries within its soul a knowledge of the nature of the higher world, one may see that it would feel no need to weep at the passing of the Buddha into a higher and better life. Perhaps the cat, like many other occultists, has been misunderstood. The point of Agrippa's motto is that only one who is centred in himself may understand the world aright, for the outer world is itself a manifestation of the inner.

In the occult tradition, the inner and the outer are aspects of the same thing, and in the cat we witness the perfect balance of inner and outer. The cat is centred in itself, while that other friend of man, the dog, attempts to find its centre in the outer world. The union of these two – like the union of a centripetal and centrifugal force – might produce only a hybrid without constancy or centre. Perhaps this is the idea behind the mediaeval belief that hybrids were not allowed into the Ark, and that the hyena was produced after the Deluge as a result of a cross between the cat and the dog. In the mediaeval lore, the hyena is neither male nor female, nor is it Christian or pagan, for it is centred neither in the outer nor the inner world. Like the cat, however, the eyes of the hyena have magic power, for there is in its eye a stone ('also called a Yena', the mediaeval text informs us) which is said to enable a person to foresee the future whensoever he places it under his tongue. The hyena must have inherited this magical eye from the cat, for the eye of the dog has no mystery or power, while the eye of the cat is preserved in an aspic of magic as old as history. The cat would seem to need a special eye, for it is so well centred within itself that it needs a powerful lens to peer outwards into the world: no wonder the same mediaeval bestiaries insist that the eyes of the cat emit their own light, which helps them see into the world. When one looks into the face of a cat one has a strange feeling that there is indeed a powerful spirit behind its eyes: and even if this notion is fanciful, it may well be the reason why the cat has been for so many centuries the symbol of wisdom, for the men of old did not choose their symbols by hazard.

The mediaeval writers of the bestiaries – the zoological lore derived from ancient times – believed that the word 'cat' came from a Latin word meaning 'acute' (*catus*), 'so acutely does she glare that her eye pierces through the shades of darkness as though with a gleam of light'. One of the standard texts dealing with the cat insists that its name is 'mouser' (*musto*) because 'she is fatal to mice'. It is 'cat', we are told, 'only in common speech', and the same text produces another etymology for the

Fig. 6   Cat after a bird, and a cat with a rat – mediaeval bestiary illustration from a manuscript in the Bodleian Library, Oxford

word, suggesting that it is from *captura* because she 'catches' things, or from *captat* because the cat lies in wait for mice or birds. The delightful illustration in the Bodleian bestiary (figure 6) shows a cat so tired of waiting that it thrusts its paw into the bird-cage, and another, having caught a mouse, using it something in the manner of a divining rod, grimly preparing to dispatch it. The background decoration of stars and lunar crescents is by no means accidental, as almost all the contemporaries of the mediaeval illuminator who painted this lovely illustration would have known that the cat was ruled by the moon. These mediaeval etymologies and origins are quite fanciful, yet there is no awkwardness in proposing two quite different names for the feline, one describing how she deals with mice in the outer world, the other relating to the light within her being.

An earlier illustration from the Ashmolean collection may well be one of the earliest pictures of a domesticated cat. He sits between a porcupine and a rabbit, below an elephant and above what may be a lion and a dog, marking the creation of the animals on the fifth day of God's labours. It is pleasant to think that the cat might have been created domesticated and tamed. Some occultists maintain that none of the animals was originally savage, but fell into savagery because of the shortcomings of mankind.

There is more than a poetic fancy in the idea that a cat should have at least two names – one which is the name of the outer cat, and one which is the secret name of its inner being. T. S. Eliot's *Old Possum's Book of Practical Cats* has gained much fame in recent years through the stage version *Cats*, even though a few of the esoteric references in the poems appear to have been missed in the production. In the poem 'The Naming of Cats' Eliot muses on the notion that cats have three names, the last of which is one 'that no human research can discover' – the one which the cat alone knows. Eliot plays with the fancy that when a cat is in a state of profound meditation, it is actually engaged on the contemplation of its true name, like a fakir or Buddhist wrapt in meditation of the powers beyond the navel. According to this poem, then, there are three names: there is the ordinary name, the personalized name and the 'deep and inscrutable singular Name'. How do these correspond to the occult tradition, with which Eliot was so familiar?

The ordinary name 'that the family uses daily' is fairly obvious – this is the 'world name' by which the cat is identified on the material plane. Yet there is a second name, also known to humans, which is more 'peculiar, and more dignified'. This is the name which allows the cat to keep its tail perpendicular and to spread out its whiskers and cherish its pride. Eliot gives some amusing versions of these names, such as Munkustrap and Jellyorum, but I suppose that 'Pyewacket' is such a name, and perhaps one of the most famous cat names of this order is 'Foss', used by the great nineteenth-century humorist Edward Lear for his own feline companion (figure 7).

The distinction between the first and second names of the cat are not really all that obvious. We may not find it easy to distinguish between the two forms unless we have some understanding of an occult theosophical teaching with which Eliot was familiar, for the poet is actually referring to a genuine occult notion. The second name, which keeps the cat's tail perpendicular (pointing to heaven) corresponds to a special stage of animal development recognized by occultists and called 'individualization'.

Occultists say that only five animals may be 'individualized'. These are the horse, the monkey, the elephant, the dog and, of course, the cat. Only these animals, occultists argue, have such an inner nature that they respond to human affection in a manner which influences the whole of

Fig. 7 'Foss, a 'untin' – a pen drawing by Edward Lear of his pet cat, Foss, from a series of heraldic blazons. This famous pet lived to the age of seventeen, and was buried with an inscribed headstone in the garden of Lear's rented villa at San Remo

their destiny in a way quite impossible with other animals. This view of individualization is rooted in the teaching of what occultists term 'the Group Soul' – in the notion that, unlike humans, animals do not normally have an individual ego which survives death. The occultists have always maintained that the higher element in humanity, which has had different names at different times, is indestructible and survives even death.

This higher element, which at the moment we call the 'ego', is of such a nature that it periodically incarnates into a physical body, with a view to gaining experience of the material plane. At death, the ego sloughs off the lower body (as well as the spiritual sheaths which make it possible for it to dwell in that body) and retains the essence of what it has learned in the preceding incarnation. For a long while the ego will remain in the spiritual realms, but it will eventually undertake to descend into matter again. It does this retaining much of its original ego and the transformed knowledge which it had attained in previous incarnations. During the whole of this process there is a sense in which the ego's own individuality remains sacrosanct and inviolate.

Now this is not normally the death process of animals, for they have Group Souls, rather than individual egos. Put simply, this means that according to the secret tradition, animals who live on the earth plane are united as one on the spiritual plane. The teaching of the Group Soul portrays the spiritual life of the animal as existing in a large and undifferentiated matrix on the astral plane. From this matrix individual rays are projected down into the earth plane to 'ensoul' the bodies of individual animals of the same type. Thus, for example, there is a feline Group Soul, from which proceeds all the rays which make up the different bodies of all the world's cats of a particular species. The individual animal is a sort of spark or 'fission' derived from the Group Soul, and still spiritually linked with it.

The most immediate consequence of this Group Soul existence for most animals is that they have not only a different quality of life from humans, but also a different kind of death. When a human dies, it is as though the material realms are sloughed off, and the permanent ego withdraws from the earth plane for a while. When an animal dies, there is normally no permanent ego to withdraw, and the individual experiences of that animal are absorbed back into the Group Soul. Nothing is lost in this animal 'death', of course, for what the animal has experienced enriches the Group Soul, but there is no longer any sense of 'individuality' for the deceased animal.

The occult teaching of 'individualization' implies that some animals are not absorbed back into the Group Soul in the usual way. Under certain circumstances the cat, the dog, the horse, the monkey and the elephant may after death carry back into the spiritual realms a sense of what might be called 'selfhood'. One has to be careful with these words, for it is not correct to suggest that an animal may develop an ego in the same sense that the human has an ego, yet it is certainly true to say that certain animals may become individualized.

In the books which attempt to present in simple images the complex notions of occultism, this idea of Group Souls is often expressed in a diagram which resembles a human hand, the fingers of which symbolize those animals which have emerged from the Group Soul (the hand itself) and live for a while in the continuum of space and time. In this continuum they gain knowledge of the world, experience especially human love and hate, yet at no time feel themselves separate as spiritual entities from the Group Soul to which they belong. If we imagine such a cat 'Group Soul' hand reflected in the waters which represent the material world, then we may represent to ourselves the notion that when the cat dies, and is absorbed back into the Group Soul, then something is left behind on the earth plane to continue with an existence of its own. Naturally, I do not talk of 'ghosts' or 'shades', which exist on a different plane (as will be seen in the section on the Psychic Cat in Chapter 4), but of the inner reality of the cat, of that element which we might truly call the 'everlasting' cat, in the same sense that we might call human beings everlasting.

The process of individualizing takes place through contact with human beings. If an animal is loved in the right way it develops a sense of individualization – it becomes 'tame', which is to say that it separates itself from the 'wild' state which is natural to the incarnate elements of a Group Soul. Again, we have to be careful in our choice of words, for to 'love in the right way' is not to 'love in a romantic way, or excessively'. According to the occult lore, true love is concerned with establishing a free relationship with the object loved. The occultists maintain that it is possible to love even an animal in the wrong way. This is true, because premature individualization is not necessarily a good thing, as the keynote to all evolution is natural growth: it is really only the human race which has the capability of speeding up its own evolutionary rate by means of disciplines and meditative practices.

However, the fact remains that according to the occult lore the cat is one of these special creatures which is being individualized, and which therefore has a destiny quite different from that of the majority of animals, and we should not be surprised to find this idea expressed in the symbols behind literature and art. Most of Aesop's fables contain a secret wisdom well beyond the level of the morals attached to them, and some of this wisdom seems to reach even into the occult notion of individualization.

The tale of the Cat and the Fox is almost transparent in its esoteric wisdom, and relates directly to the idea of individualization. While out walking one day, the cat meets the fox, who begins to boast about his cleverness, about what he calls his 'hundred tricks'. The cat smiles knowingly, and says, 'I have only one trick.' Just at that moment, a pack of hounds bursts on the scene. The fox speeds off, pursued by the hounds, and the cat, practising her 'one trick', leaps into the safety of the tree (Plate 1). One by one, the fox tries each of his hundred tricks, attempting every means he knows to evade the hounds. However, at length he runs out of tricks, and is hunted down. Meanwhile, the cat sits secure in the tree, watching the end of her boastful companion.

For all his street-wise cunning, the fox is always lost, no matter how

Fig. 8   The lunar grin of the disappearing Cheshire Cat: Tenniel's illustration from
Alice in Wonderland

many tricks he uses to preserve his life, for in the end he is swallowed up
as an individual into his Group Soul. The fox is not one of those animals
chosen for individualization in the present evolution of the world. The
cat, on the other hand, climbs safe and secure into the higher part of the
world (the tree) and watches the tumult below as a fully fledged individual. Perhaps this is one reason why the engraving by Tenniel of the
vanishing cat (figure 8) high in its tree is such an enduring image: it is an
image which speaks directly to our unconscious, just like the story retold
by Aesop. Like the eyes of the cat, the body of the cat also waxes and
wanes, as with all earthly things; yet the individuality of the Cheshire
cat remains secure, as the everlasting cat. The grin of the cat is the symbol of the eternal spirit which is periodically 'hung' on the tree, which is
the physical body enmeshed for a while in space and time.

Yet another tale told by Aesop – that of the Cat and the Cock – takes us
into a deeper level of esoteric symbolism. The cat pounces on a cock (figure 4) and then casts about for an excuse to eat him. The excuse is a very
weak one: 'You make an awful din at night by crowing and keeping
folks awake, therefore I shall eat you.' The poor cock argues that he

crows to ensure that men are up early to do their day's work, and that the world is very much in need of him as an alarm clock. 'Even so,' says the cat, brushing aside all reasoning, 'I intend to eat you' – and she does.

The story points to the most ancient layer of occult symbolism in the world – the antithesis between soul and spirit, and the esoteric notion that Man needs to wake up in a spiritual sense. The cat is ruled by the Moon, and is therefore a symbol of soul-life, while the cock is ruled by the Sun, and is a symbol of spirit-life. This cat is not concerned with humans, while the cock is. When there is no love, the soul-life submerges the spirit-life: when there is no love, then, allegorically speaking, the Moon puts out the Sun. It is the cyclical history of mankind in a feline nutshell allegory. Aesop's story contains an important occult message: that the cat must learn to love humanity – which is to say that humanity must make itself worthy of feline love.

Long ago I came to the conclusion that the ancient mythology contains a wisdom which is often overlooked in modern times. Individualization is to do with love, and Venus, who is the goddess of love, is the one who in the ancient myths is transformed into a cat. The stories of goddesses being transformed into cats, and cats into goddesses, seem to point to the occult notion of love leading to a sort of spiritual isolation from the Group Souls. One is reminded of the old story attributed to Aesop, though seemingly older even than his strain of story-telling, about the goddess Venus and the cat who had fallen in love with a handsome man. The cat implored the goddess to change her into a beautiful woman that she might marry the man. Venus did as the cat asked, and once she had been transformed she became the wife of the man. Venus herself was ever concerned with the outer form of things – with the beauty of the physical body, rather than with the beauty of soul – and one day she decided to test whether her magic had worked internally as much as externally. She caused a mouse to run through the bedroom while the young couple were in bed. The transformed cat could not forget her true nature, and she pushed aside the bedcothes and leapt in pursuit of the mouse (Plate 2). Venus, realizing that her magic was only surface deep, changed the woman back into her former state. The moral is clear – we all wish to be something which we are not, but few of us have the inner resources to deal with changes which we wish upon ourselves. When we look into the lore of the cat, we see that in truth the gods have helped to transform the animal into a human state, even though that change is not so dramatic or immediate as in the Aesop fable.

Slowly the cat is being humanized by the power of human love – only by such a process may the inner change be as radical and convincing as the outer.

I doubt that it is possible for us to find out why the cat is such an extraordinary creature, at once centred in its own being yet at the same time clearly enmeshed in the spiritual realm. The answer to such a question belongs to levels of thinking not normally available to man. But what man has woven around the cat – the symbolism of the cat, as opposed to the cat itself – is quite a different thing. The symbolism of the cat reflects this strange union of the centred spiritual being, and has resulted in a most extraordinary collection of arcane beliefs, symbols and notions about the cat and its inner meaning. It is a symbolism so varied and contradictory that it can encompass the cat as sign of the Virgin Mary (figure 9) and the cat as symbol of the Devil – its mythology is so extensive that it stretches from Egypt, where the cat was deified as a creature of the stars (Plate 4), to England of the sixteenth century where it was demoted to the rank of demon (Plate 22), and then, two centuries later, returned by the new mythology of science to the stars. The one thing which all these divergent images and mythologies proclaim is that the cat is an extraordinary creature, carrying within its inner being a world of different meanings, from the esoteric to the banal.

Like the human beings who love or hate her, the cat was originally a creature of the stars, but fell earthwards to become a materialistic symbol of a hellish nightmare. This is why the form of this book may so conveniently be divided into two parts, one of which deals with the Cat of the Stars, the other with the Fallen Cat. The cat of the stars is (like many modern human beings) just awakening, as to a new dawn in which she finds herself what she has always been, in spite of the calumny attached to her name and history – a cat which will last for ever: this is why I call the first section of the book The Everlasting Cat. In contrast, the cat of the demons has had an unfair destiny, doomed to a reputation it has not deserved; yet the many legends and myths about this damned feline race require a special treatment in the second section, under the general title of The Hellish Cat.

Each of these different cats has its own fascination and secret history, and the cat herself seems happy in both roles, for she is the mediator, the true initiate, who can dwell in the higher and the lower worlds simultaneously. The vision of the cat as a being who is conversant at once with the world of man and with the world of spirits is nowhere more graphi-

Fig. 9   Cat linked with the symbolism of the Virgin Mary in Baroccio's Madonna of
the Cat *in the National Gallery, London. This symbolism is directly derived from
Egyptian feline imagery: within such a context the cat is often interpreted as a symbol
of virginity*

cally told than in the great Finnish national epic of the *Kalevala*. The hero
Lemminkainen, a jovial if reckless individual, is involved in a magical
adventure with a giant cat which draws a sledge over the snows and
carries some men to the realm of the evil spirits, called Pohjola. 'Thus,'
says the epic, 'Lemminkainen mocked at young men, old men, and men
in the prime of life, by means of incantations.' This magical cat of the
Kalevala is adopted as the symbol of the intermediary between the world
of men and the world of the dark unknown. We shall see much the same
feline symbolism attached to the Egyptian god Thoth, the greatest of all
the intermediaries, who stood between man and his wisdom, between
man and the spiritual which he must traverse after death.

No wonder the mediaeval bestiary would link one name of the cat
with a 'light within', and say that her other name was connected with
death and killing.

PART I

The Everlasting Cat

Chapter One

THE MAGICAL EYE

Why are Freya's
Eyes so sharp?
From her eyes it seems
That fire doth burn.

Quoted by I D A M E L L E N from the *Elder Edda*

In mythology, the cat's eyes are more intense than humans' because they see into the higher and lower realms: it is, as the verse quoted above from an old Norse poem suggests, as though fire burns from those all-seeing eyes. In classical Greek mythology the lynx (which, as we shall see, was sacred to the northern goddess Freya) was said to have the ability to see through stone walls. The truth is that, while in reality the lynx's eyes are somewhat less powerful than mythology would have them, they are still capable of quite remarkable vision. In 1950 the naturalist Lindemann published experimental material showing that his own tame lynx could see a mouse at 75 metres, and a roe deer at half a kilometre.

In his personal memoirs, *Facing the Big Cats*, the trainer Clyde Beatty records how on a first night in Montreal, as he was exhibiting his skills with a cage full of lions and tigers, the lights in the circus failed. The darkness was no problem for the beasts, for their eyes were so acute of vision that they could see perfectly well. Beatty himself was in a quandary, for he could not see the animals at all. At all costs, he had to avoid letting them know that he was unable to see clearly: he knew that the 'advantage' of their sight against his blindness was all they would need to induce them to attack him. His instinct as a trainer gave him a sense that he should not disturb the sequence of the act, for this would enrage the animals: he somehow continued with the normal sequence in the darkness, directing mainly by means of feel and expertise, and in this way managed to fool the animals and continue the act until temporary light had been rushed to him. Anyone without Beatty's knowledge of feline sight and sense of rhythm would have been mauled to death in that cage.

The iris of the cat's eye is capable of adjusting to a wide range of different lighting conditions, and variations in lighting visibly affect the appearance of the eyes. In bright light, the pupil is little more than a vertical slit, while in the darkness it expands almost to the full extent of the iris. This capacity for adjusting to change in light, which is aided by a special relationship of rods and cones in the retina, has given rise to the popular belief that cats can 'see in the dark', which is not strictly true. In his wonderful collection of popular fallacies (not a few of which concern cats) Ackermann comments especially on this opinion that cats can see in the dark, and quotes an entertaining story reported in the *Daily Telegraph* for 12 March 1941. It seems that someone suggested that the best way for the Royal Air Force to tackle the problem of night-flying enemy bombers during the early days of the Second World War was to furnish each British aeroplane gunner with a cat. The idea was that the gunner should then aim his gun in the direction in which the cat was looking, in the certainty that he would bring down the enemy machine.

The proposal is perhaps no more absurd than many of the 'spells' and 'charms' recorded in Owen Wood's *Alphabetical book of Physicall Secrets* of 1639, which includes a recipe for curing bad sight in 'eyes that have Pearle or Web'. 'Take all the head of a black cat,' writes this occult Mrs Beeton, burn this head to ashes, and then, with the aid of a quill, blow the dust into the sick eye three times a day. Afterwards, put on the eyes some oak leaves doubled together and wetted with rosewater. 'Renew as need requireth. It cureth,' he concludes. The spell may be a load of nonsense by modern standards, yet it is an example of the extent to which the cat was linked with the eye in terms of occult belief. Even the natural historian Topsell left minute directions as to how one might use the head of a black cat to remedy loss of eyesight. The colour of the cat presumably symbolized the darkness around the head of the person who was to be cured. Less macabre is the Cornish charm which involved 'stroking' a blinding stye with the end of a black cat's tail. Not surprisingly, the hairs were to be drawn over the afflicting stye nine times – the number relating to the secret power of the cat and its alleged number of lives.

The link between sight and the cat no doubt arises from what we now call 'sympathetic magic', based on the ancient idea that things of a like nature are mystically connected. According to some mythologists, the eye of the cat was supposed to have been one of the eyes of the Egyptian god Horus, looking down from the skies – since the Sun itself was his other eye, we must assume that this cat-eye was the Moon. We may take it from this that at least some ancient Egyptians held the conceit that, at times, there was in the skies an enormous cat (presumably as black as the night sky) peering down at the world. In other Egyptian systems, which passed into the western tradition by way of the hermetic texts, the Moon is the left eye and the Sun the right eye of the god Horus, or of Isis and Horus respectively, and, indeed, of other gods in which the feline and the anthropomorphic mingle. The 'waxing and waning' of the cat's pupil does in some way resemble the growing and diminishing of the Moon's rotund face as it moves in its monthly cycle around the earth. In one of his more memorable poems, W. B. Yeats writes of the black cat Minnaloushe, 'the nearest kin of the moon', the pure light of which troubled his animal blood.

> Does Minnaloushe know that his pupils
> Will pass from change to change,
> And that from round to crescent
> From crescent to round they range?

So far was sight linked with the cat in mediaeval magical recipes that the formula for producing the famous 'Hand of Glory' – favoured by thieves who were convinced that it would confer invisibility upon them – involved the use of a cat's fat. The hand itself had to be cut from the right arm of a hanged murderer during the eclipse of the Moon, while the candle which was inserted into this grisly fragment was made from the fat of the dead man, or from the grease and fat of a black tom-cat. That which when living had perfect sight, was presumed when dead to convey such bad vision that those in the same room would not be able to see the owner of the Hand of Glory.

If we flick through the magical books of the late Middle Ages – those reservoirs of superstitions which are still part and parcel of vulgar belief – we learn that cats can see in the dark, that cats can see ghosts, and will mewl at the sight of the demons invisible to man, that cats' eyes are so powerful that they are used in southern Negro voodoo charms, and that one may tell the state of the tide from the size of the cat's pupils, on the principle that when the pupils are narrow, it is low tide, when they are wide, the tide is high. The list mingles vestiges of the old beliefs in the power of the Moon with the ancient Egyptian tradition of the cat as a confronter and destroyer of the demon or serpent of darkness (Plate 4).

As we have seen, it is not too fanciful to trace a connexion between the ancient Egyptian symbol Ru ◊ which appears in many of the magical texts with the image of the curious form of the cat's eye. Ru meant many things, but almost all are connected with the notion of passage from one space into another: it is a drawing of a 'doorway', and of the vaginal passage of birth, through which creatures slide from the spiritual realm into the material plane. This strange door symbol is preserved even in the modern symbol for woman ♀, a symbol also used to denote the archetype woman Venus in astrological symbolism. Specialists tell us that the origin of this symbol was not (as we might expect) a mirror, held in the hands of the eternal Venusian woman, but a combination of the Ru and the Tau cross. It is relevant to our theme that the old idea of birth and of woman are both related to a symbol which is almost certainly linked with the cat's eyes. This explains why for centuries the 'cat's eye stone' (mentioned in the mediaeval occult manuscripts) has been used as an amulet, and why the cat was sacred to women in the ancient Egyptian cults. This female connexion (and indeed the idea of spiritual birth) was preserved in those early Christian pictures which show the Virgin or the Child playing with a cat. We shall examine the secret symbolism behind such images in Chapter 3.

The connexion between the cat and birth has afforded many strange superstitions, but perhaps the most striking is the one which has cropped up from time to time in one form or another in the Scottish courts. Until comparatively recently it was believed in parts of Scotland that if a male cat chanced to jump over food, then any woman who ate that food could conceive cats. It seems that the belief postulated that the jumping cat could discharge feline semen on to the food, and it was this which made the woman pregnant. An example is recorded on 5 March 1654, when Jean Simpson of Rothiemay, Scotland, had confessed at a meeting of the Sessions that she and her mother visited a wise woman to obtain herbs to abort the kittens known to be in her belly. The doctors and churchmen refused to allow her herbal potions to stem the unwanted pregnancy, saying that it was a child and not cats. Had kittens indeed been born to the young lady, it is likely that she would have achieved some fame – as it was, after this reference she disappears completely from history.

The magical power of the Egyptian Udjat is widely recognized by occultists and mythologists, and it is not surprising to find it linked in many ways with the sacred cat. The Udjat is the 'Eye of Horus, the Sun God' in popular mythology, but its actual history points to its being something more than merely a deified eye. Horus was the king-god whose eyes were associated with the luminaries – his right eye with the Sun, his left eye with the Moon. Something of this 'left' and 'right' symbolism was preserved in the use of the two lions posted couchant on either side of the large solar symbol of Horus, the sun-god, in many Egyptian drawings and paintings. The lion to the left was symbolic of the past, the lion to the right of the future, so that we may take it that one was a solar lion and the other a lunar lion. There is evidence to show that the two lion-heads which are found on the celestial throne of Mary in later Christian symbolism, and which are conventionally associated with the 'Lion of Judah', were actually derived from this solar symbolism of 'past' and 'future' to represent eternity, a state 'out of time', beyond the limitations of past and future.

It appears that in later Egyptian art forms, the solar eye was considered to be an attribute of the Sun-god Ra, while the lunar eye alone was given to Horus. The evil Set stole this lunar eye, but finding no use for it, he threw it to the ground, breaking it into pieces. The eye was found by Thoth (the Egyptian mystery god, the equivalent of the later Hermes), who had the ability to make it whole again. Thoth as the healer, Horus as the blinded god, Set as the evil serpent, and the image of an eye, 'the Eye of Horus', which was once whole, then fragmented, then made whole again: it is the story of man's own spiritual vision which is fragmented at birth (when he emerges through the passage of birth, through the realm of the Moon) and so blinded to the higher world, and must have his vision restored by the secret lore of the wise man knowledgeable in the hermetic praxis. Besides the connexion with the Moon, what has this story to do with the Egyptian cat, or even with the Egyptian goddess Bastet?

The answer may never be fully told in modern times, yet there are tantalizing survivals from the Egyptian world to show that the Udjat and the cat are intimately linked in magical beliefs. Very many Egyptian sacred eye amulets incorporate tiny images of cats into the 'decorative' registers of the Udjat or sit upon the symbol (figure 10). An example

Fig. 10 Egyptian cat sitting upon a box inscribed with the Udjat symbol. Artwork after the funerary papyrus of Nespeheran, in the Bodleian Library, Oxford

from the Flinders Petrie Collection of University College, London, has nineteen tiny cats sitting in two rows above and below the main eye. The most perfect of all Egyptian cat statues, that of Bastet in the British Museum, London (figure 3), has a protective amulet of the Udjat around its neck as well as the scarabæus beetle on its forehead.

What is this feline Udjat symbolism, so deeply involved with the mythology of Ra and Horus, and with the reconstitution of vision by the hermetic art? It is the eternal story, expressed through the feline nature.

The cat is possessed of a vision which can penetrate with ease into those higher realms which are unavailable to men who have not participated in the hermetic mysteries.

In the funerary papyrus of Nespeheran in the Bodleian Library (figure 10), the cat sits upon a box which bears the single image of the Udjat, the seeing eye which (curiously enough) is the single right eye of the god. Are the occultists wrong in claiming that this Udjat is a symbol of the so-called 'third eye', that organ of higher vision which is as yet undeveloped in ordinary men? The ancient Oriental wisdom called this third eye a Chakra, one of the 'organs' or points of energy on the astral body of man, and located it on the forehead, between the two physical eyes. Is there any relevance in the fact that the scarabæus beetle (the 'resurrection' symbol) on the bronze Gayer-Anderson Cat is in the middle of its fore-

Fig. 11   The Egyptian cat-headed Sekhmet, with kittens at her feet and in her sistrum (right hand). British Museum

head (figure 3)? Is this cat a symbol of what all men might become –
transformed recipients of a higher vision?

The Egyptian goddess Sekhmet was the 'Great Cat', sometimes called
'Mau', and a thousand Egyptian sculptures present her with the inscrutable head of a cat (figure 11). As with her little sister Bubastis, there is a
connexion with fire in the mythology of Sekhmet, for she is called the
'fire and lioness' goddess, and it was she who destroyed the evil snake
god Apep with fire. Apep was the Lord of the Power of Darkness, the
Egyptian equivalent of the Zoroastrian Angri Mainyu, the prototype of
our own Satan. Sekhmet is on the side of the angels, therefore, in attacking Apep, and she is linked with the Moon – that satellite which in the
early astrological texts is said to be the planet which has rule over
women and cats.

It is not surprising that, in a culture which has such an important cat-
god as Sekhmet, there should have been a system of taboos and beliefs
that protected and even worshipped the cat, and which appears to have
produced the first domestic cats that spread (probably much earlier than
is generally realized) into Europe and, eventually, the rest of the world.
The cat was held in such veneration by the Egyptians that they
mummified the bodies of their dead pets as though they were holy
things. During the last century a cemetery of over 50,000 mummified
cats was discovered in Tel Beni-Hassan, and it was to the loss of archae-
ology and natural history that this ancient burial ground was rifled and
the bodies destroyed.

Another reflection of the almost superstitious awe in which the cat
was held in Egyptian times was the custom for those in whose house a
cat had died to shave their eyebrows. The soft hair of the eyebrows was
shaved away not merely as an outer sign that the household had lost its
pet, but also in sympathetic magic, for the eyebrows resembled the fur of
the lost creature, and were crescents in form – the ancient symbol of the
Moon.

In Egyptian times the cat was a lunar symbol, sacred to the goddess
Isis; it is for this reason that one sometimes sees the image of a cat on top
of the sistrum in the hands of that goddess. As the nineteenth-century
occultist Gerald Massey records, 'The eye of the cat . . . seems to follow
the lunar phases in its growth and decline, and its orbs shine like two
stars in the darkness of night.' This ancient belief is sometimes given as
the reason why later mythologies present the lunar goddess Diana as
taking the shape of a cat when seeking to escape the sexual attentions of

Typhon. However, the truth is that Diana and Isis (from whom the former was born) were the most important of the lunar goddesses, and it was natural to link both with the sacred image of the cat.

The Ru-form of the ankh and the eye-based Udjat were not the only feline-derived symbols in Egyptian art. Many of the traditions attached to the use of magical stones, the 'gamalei' of mediaeval lore, are derived from Egyptian beliefs connected with the magical power of the cat's eye. That there should be a cat-stone (sometimes named in the Latin *cati oculus*, sometimes in the Greek *pledopoly*) is not really surprising, for many magical stones were connected with bestiaries, such as the toad-stone, the eagle-stone, the swallow-stone and the cock-stone, all of which entered the magical pharmacopoeia of the Middle Ages, each with their specific properties linked by invisible yet powerful virtues with the creature for which it was named.

In many of the mediaeval 'gem' books we find the cat's-eye stone mentioned as being a most efficacious amulet, for the stone is supposed to protect the wearer from all the evils of witchcraft. The Egyptologist E. A. Wallis Budge tells us that the Arabs claimed the stone had power to make its owner invisible in battle, and he records the story of how in some regions, when a man was about to go on a long journey and doubted his wife's fidelity, he induced her to drink milk in which the cat's-eye stone had been washed. This magical milk was not supposed to enforce fidelity, but rather to ensure that no children would be born of the adulterous liaison.

This 'cat's eye' is really a gem with a changeable lustre, but it is often confused with the yellowish-green 'precious stone' called the chrysoberyl. Again, the cat's-eye stone (properly called the 'cat's eye') is not always distinguished from the 'Cater's Eye', a dull red stone with a white mark on it, not unreasonably claimed to symbolize the pupil of the cat's eye. This particular stone is rarely worn as an amulet for it has a bad reputation. Some authors claim that it is to be used by those intent on causing strife between people.

Adopting cat's eyes for the purposes of magic is not limited to the ancient world. Their strange lunar shape has been used to great effect in the modern art of the cartoon film. Generally speaking, when artists seek to 'humanize' animals in making cartoon films, they make their eyes as human as possible. This practice presents something of a problem when humanizing a cat, but usually the artist ignores the slit-iris of the genuine feline in favour of the round iris of the human being. Like most cats drawn in the humorous tradition or in cartoon style, Tom of the famous *Tom and Jerry* cartoons usually has eyes of the human variety. However, when there is a wish to present Tom in a particularly evil mood, the artist may resort to the slit- iris, which helps to make the face almost demonic.

This artistic licence is not entirely modern. Many artists who specialize in painting animals tend to 'humanize' cats' eyes – particularly when painting adorable little kittens. A fine example of this is in the eighteenth-century feline idyll by Pyon Sang-Byok (figure 12), which shows two cats in pursuit of sparrows. The painting is masterly in the way it captures the sinuous feline rhythms and fur-texture of the cats, and it is most interesting to observe how the pupils of the 'adorable kitten' which appears to be stuck half way up the tree-trunk have been humanized.

The cat is the most endearing emblem of the Moon, while its strange eyes are symbols of the Moon's creative and regenerative power. They

Fig. 12   Detail of silk-painting Cats and Sparrows *by Pyon Sang-Byok. Duksoo Palace Museum, Seoul*

are the slits through which spirit pours into the earthly plane, injecting into matter that powerful lunar force which in lesser men breeds lunacy and in the more sensitive souls breathes poetry and the arts. We find therefore in the eyes of the cat a number of traditions which point to the duality which deals with both the world of demonic darkness and the world of spiritual light.

This strange duality was expressed in the complex symbolism attached to the sacred cat in Egyptian times. According to the ancient papyrus records which have been made available through Budge's translations, the head of the cat is linked with the god Ra and its eyes with the snake-like Uraeus (again recalling the Buddhist legend which has the snake and the cat refusing to weep at the death of Buddha). The nose of the cat is ruled by Thoth, who is ape-headed, reminding us of the mediaeval legend which has the Moon create as her first two animals the cat and the monkey. The cat is said to have the ears of Ned-er-tcher, the mouth of Tem, the neck of Neheb-ka, the breast of Thoth, the heart of the Sun-god Ra, the belly of Osiris, the thighs of Menthu, the legs of Kensu, the feet of Amen-Horus, the haunches of Horus, the soles of the feet of Ra and the bowels of Meh-urit. Each of these associations has its own magical secrets and, even without examining these in detail, it is clear that there is no part of the cat which does not belong to the gods. Yet the most powerful aspect are the feline eyes, the portals through which the lunar spirit of imagination finds entry into the world.

Chapter Two

THE MAGICAL NAME

As with all the secret things, there is magic in the name of the cat – even in a few personal cat names – and since some of these throw light on the occult nature of the creature, it will be worth our while to glance at them. Both our modern popular words for the feline betray the magical and historical origin of the animal. 'Puss' is almost certainly from the Egyptian word *Pasht*, which was one of the names for the goddess Bastet, of whom we shall hear a great deal in this book. The simple word 'cat' came to Britain with the domestic cat itself, either with the Roman legions or with the Roman monks who brought Christianity to this land. The Romans had called the cat *felis*, which has the same root as *felix*, linked with the 'good and auspicious omen' of magical divination; but when the domestic cat became popular in Rome, as an alternative rat-catcher to the weasel, it was called, as was the weasel itself, *catta*, probably from the Nubian *kadis*. This word of Egyptian origin appears to be the root of almost all the European words, from the English to the Italian (*gatto*) and even into the Russian (*koshka*).

It is an interesting reflection on the unconscious survival of magical names that even nowadays we call after a cat with the name 'Puss', from the Egyptian goddess, rather than use the Roman 'Cat'. No self-respecting puss will answer to such a name, unless of course one rattles the feeding saucer at the same time. There are records of a humorous derivation of 'Puss' from the French *le puss*, which was supposed to come from the Latin *Lepus*, meaning 'hare'. This derivation is of course quite fanciful, yet the fact is that the word puss was used in England for both cats and hares until well into the eighteenth century. This may well be connected with the confusion between witches and hares which existed in these years. Sometimes a hare was looked on as a witch familiar (like the cat), but at other times it was regarded as being the witch herself, transformed to animal shape. So prevalent was this notion that, at the height of the English witchcraft trials, one northern farmer recorded that whenever he saw a hare running across his fields, he took it for granted that it was a witch on her way to the sabbat.

To judge from these trials, the same dramatic misinterpretation of nature must have occurred when cats were seen sleeping by the fireplace or sitting outside their owners' doors. Cats were no longer pussies, but witch-imps or demons. The old streets of King's Lynn, Norfolk, a notorious centre for witchcraft in the seventeenth century, may look peaceful to modern eyes, yet in those days the cat would not have been a cat so much as the Devil. Trial records show that there was no doubt at all in the minds of the occupants of the village of Sible Hedingham (north of Chelmsford) that the cat which wandered from house to house was a demon in disguise; and in the court hearings which record the subsequent trials for witchcraft we learn that the name given to the cat was 'Sathan', scarcely distinguished from the Satan whom he was supposed to serve.

The Puss in Boots who is striding jauntily below the statue of Perrault in the Tuileries gardens of Paris (Plate 6) seems more of a pirate than a cat. He is well dressed – overdressed, indeed – and very, very sure of himself: he seems to be aware that he is more than a fairytale cat, and that his feline ancestry goes back to the mystery wisdom. In his fascinating account of the secret mysteries of the cathedrals, Fulcanelli, intimately familiar with the methods of esoteric symbolism, points out that the fairytale Puss in Boots really belongs to the occult tradition.

Puss in Boots came to English literature from the stories told by the Italian Straparola, by way of the French *Chat Botté* (Booted Cat), a cunning cat who acquired for his poor master a royal marriage and a fortune. Within the hidden meanings of this tale we can trace the cat as symbol of the unconscious power in man, which has far greater wisdom, a far greater ability to respond to the call of destiny, than our conscious mind. Just as the cat of occult lore is linked with the power of the Moon, so indeed is the unconscious in man. Even in modern times you will find that popular books on astrology relate the Moon in the horoscope chart to the unconscious or subconscious – which is to say, to those powers within man which act by means which are hidden from the light of the conscious mind. The jaunty Puss in Boots is the unconscious wisdom which lifts the foolish master from his peasant world into the ideal realm of kings and queens, enabling him to find his princess and take her as his wife. We shall examine this Italianate French cat at a later point, but it is worth observing here that the theme appears in a variety of different stories and myths, and is to some extent mixed up with the account, dramatized annually in the pantomimes, of how Richard Whittington became the Lord Mayor of London, and married his rich master's daughter, after turning back to London with his faithful cat. Meanwhile the *Chat Botté* (pronounced shabottey) is a phrase which in the secret or 'green' language of the occultists is said to refer to the Chabot or Sabot, a French word for a humming-top. It seems that in the mediaeval period it was customary for the choirboys to whip such tops down the aisles of Langres cathedral in a rite known as the 'Flagellation of the Alleluia'. The Sabot top was said to be a humming top, which had painted or incised on its flat surface a cross or a Tau, part of the ankh symbolism we have already noted in connexion with the cat (pages 4 and 26).

Such customs and processions as are recorded for Langres, of which the most notorious was the 'Feast of the Fools' with its Mad Mother (who may have been Perrault's original Mother Goose), gave rise to very many curious words and symbols which are now imperfectly remembered in fairy stories or are preserved in the secret symbolism of ecclesiastical carvings of gargoyles and misericords. It is no accident that some of the secret symbols on church towers, and one or two gargoyles, are portrayed with the whiskered face of a cat. Is this diabolic association the reason for the (now dying) taboo which some communities have of saying the word cat out loud? It is claimed that the black cats favoured by seafaring men are never referred to while on board ship save by some euphemism.

Even the personal names of cats carry their own occult mystery. 'Grimalkin' was the name used in earlier times for an old she-cat – especially for a wicked-looking one such as might reasonably be associated with a witch imp. The word is derived from a combination of 'grey' and 'malkin', the latter of which is said to be a diminutive of the female name Matilda, apparently used as a generic name for an untidy slut, a scarecrow or a grotesque puppet. Interestingly enough, the same name was often given to the pagan Queen of the May, who had overtones of the 'old religion' or witchcraft in her bones.

DOROTHEA: You must turn tippet
And suddenly, and truly, and discreetly,
Put on the shape of order and humanity,
Or you must marry Malkyn, the May-lady . . .

write Beaumont and Fletcher in their play *Monsieur Thomas* (II, ii). The
Matilda or Malkin name is now changed to 'Marian', for the May-lady is
the village girl who is crowned Queen of the May. The name has become
that of Maid Marion, Robin Hood's lover, and it has also entered into the
Morris dances, though more often than not this Malkin is now disguised
as a man. By the time Shakespeare wrote his witchcraft play *Macbeth*, the
word Grimalkin was used for the familiar. 'I come, Graymalkin,' says
the First Witch, following her cat, which (as any Elizabethan would
know) was really a demon in disguise.

FIRST WITCH: I come, Graymalkin!
ALL: Paddock calls.

Is Paddock the name for a cat, also? The answer is no, for 'paddock' is a
diminutive of the Anglo-Saxon word 'pad', which means toad. 'As cold
as a paddock' might in modern times be taken as referring to an open
field, but in reality it meant 'as cold as a toad'. Reginald Scot, who wrote
about witchcraft in the sixteenth century in the hope that he might
dispel some of the witchcraft delusions, points out that the toad is next
in popularity to the cat as a witch's familiar. 'Some say they can keep
divels and spirits in the likeness of todes and cats . . . But . . . the tode is
the most excellent object, whose ouglie deformitie signifieth sweete and
amiable fortune: in respect whereof some superstitious wiches preserve
todes for their familiars.'

   The cat and the toad are therefore the two popular symbols of the
witch familiar, and it is interesting that we should find the toad on one
side of the humanoid head of the terrible demon king Bael and the cat's
head on the other. I often wonder if Shakespeare had this image of Bael
in mind when he spoke of a demonic cat and a demonic toad in those
two lines of his dramatic opening to *Macbeth*.

   Scot finds himself interested in why the most infamous witch trial
judge of the sixteenth century, Jean Bodin, should insist that all cats are
witches in disguise. With tongue in cheek, Scot writes, 'Whie witches are
turned into cats [Bodin] alledgeth no reason, and therefore . . . I saie,

that witches are curst queanes, and manie times scratch one another, or their neighbours by the faces; and therefor perchance are turned into cats. But I have put twentie of these witchmongers to silence with this one question; to wit, Whether a witch that can turne a woman into a cat, etc. can also turne a cat into a woman?' In passing we might note with pleasure Scot's delightful phrase 'witches are curst queanes': Scot was a fine scholar, and he knew full well that the cat was once loved and worshipped as the Queen of Heaven, even if he was not familiar with the full tradition of the Egyptian goddess Bubastis. It was a derivative of this Queen which gave us the Queen of May, that in turn gave us the name Marion and also the word 'Grimalkin'. And so the words circulate, obscuring in the changes they ring the fact that the cat is a fallen spirit of heaven.

We shall find later that there is a deeper meaning in the traditional image of the cat-headed Bael than would at first appear, for esoteric symbolism insists that the left side of the demon is cold, as one might expect from a 'paddock', while the right side is warm or hot. This latter notion, which links the cat with heat, is directly derived from the Egyptian lore which views the cat-headed Sekhmet as a goddess of Fire. Even the demonic feline images (Plate 7) cannot obscure the fact that our creature was once a goddess.

The Egyptian origin of the cat has received at least one arcane notice in modern times in the delightful verses of Don Marquis, who writes of the cat Mehitabel and her acquaintance Archie who was once a verse-libre poet, now condemned to live in the insignificant body of a cockroach. The names should really be written mehitabel and archie, without capital letters, because the poems are composed by archie himself, who writes upon a typewriter, pressing the keys down by leaping upon them individually head first. He is not strong enough to operate the key-change, and therefore writes all his verse in lower-case. Perhaps an archie in the age of the word-processor might well become an Archie – but then half the fun of his verses would be lost.

This lower-case mehitabel is a firm believer in reincarnation, and claims that she once lived in ancient Egypt in the body of Cleopatra. It might be tempting to take this merely as a humorous reference to the Egyptian origin of the domestic cat (which mehitabel certainly is, for all her opinions about herself), but the choice of name is especially interesting because of its structure. If you lose the upper-case C, then you have:

leopatra   or leo patra

which is near enough to the Latin 'Leo Patria', Lion Fatherland. Alternatively you may take the word CLEOPATRA and derive from it the words LEO and CAT as well as more than a suggestion of LEOPARD. Perhaps mehitabel was not quite so superficial as she pretended to be, for the name she chose for a previous incarnation pointed both to the great antiquity of the domestic cat and to the names of its most powerful contemporary relations.

But the simple word 'cat' is not always what it seems to be. We find it used in connexion with some of the ancient standing stones, cairns or rock formations, as for example the Cat Stone near the Blackstone Edge of Lancashire. This name probably does not relate to the feline race, but more likely to the ancient word 'cot', which meant a 'dwelling'. Equally, the 'Cat Stanes' of Scotland have nothing to do with felines, for the word is from the Celtic 'cath', meaning a battle. Good examples survive in Kirkliston (West Lothian) and Kingsinch, and there is an excellent Cat Stane with related stone-lined graves near Edinburgh Airport.

As to the finger-picking twine game played by children popularly called 'cat's cradle', it probably has nothing to do with cats at all. Some authorities have suggested that this 'cat' is nothing more than a corruption of the word 'catch', which derives from the French *crèche* or manger. The connexion between this game and magic symbolism is affirmed by James Frazer in *The Golden Bough*. He records that among the Eskimos the boys are not permitted to play the game, on the assumption that it might magically induce their fingers to become entangled in the harpoon lines in later life.

Some of the personal names which we use for cats are exceedingly ancient. The name 'Mahu' used by Shakespeare for one of the demons in *King Lear* is almost certainly a throwback (by way of the demonological tradition) to the Mau of Egyptian times which, as we have seen, was one of the names for the cat-headed Bastet. (The name is also used by Sir John Suckling in his play *The Goblins* for the Devil himself and is a reminder that the cat was firmly linked with the fall of those pagan gods and goddesses who were demonized in the writings of the Christians.) I wonder if this is another of Shakespeare's double jokes, for Mahu is making the life of 'poor Tom' a misery, and even in the Bard's day Tom was the generic term for a male cat, a name now enshrined in our modern culture in the series title for those hilarious *Tom and Jerry* films. Shakespeare's subtle esoteric joke is that the female cat (Mahu) is making the life of the tomcat (Tom) unbearable.

In one of the more amusing asides in his study of facts and fables, the Reverend Brewer points out that, when the two names are contrasted, 'Jack is usually the sharp, shrewd, active fellow, and Tom the honest dullard. No one would think of calling the thick-headed male cat a Jack, nor the pert, dextrous, thieving daw a Tom. The former is almost instinctively called a Tom-cat, and the latter a Jack-daw.' Brewer was no student of the occult, and he often gets his history of magic wrong, yet in this observation (whether he knows it or not) he is on the edge of the secret lore of sound. To support his comments, he quotes a short section from a poem by Cowper, but as he could not have known the more pertinent 'Esther's Tomcat' by Ted Hughes, I will quote a line or two here myself, and recommend all cat-lovers to read the whole delightful poem,* which sets down the nature of the Tom to perfection:

> Daylong this tomcat lies stretched flat
> As an old rough mat, no mouth and no eyes.
> Continual wars and wives are what
> Have tattered his ears and battered his head.
> ...
> He leaps and lightly
> Walks upon sleep, his mind on the moon.
> Nightly over the round world of men,
> Over the roofs go his eyes and outcry.

While on the subject of cat names, we might ask what symbolism or mythology lies behind the Manx cat? How did a tailless cat find its way to the Isle of Man? One theory claims that the cat came from Tibet, where it was a temple guardian, much like the fu-dog of the Chinese (which itself appears to have cat blood mixed in with its dragon ancestry). Somehow this Tibetan cat found its way to Spain, was taken aboard a galleon of the Spanish Armada which was sunk near the Isle of Man, and from this sinking escaped and swam safely to the island. The confused travelogue is probably as good an explanation for the arrival of the tailless cat as any you will find, though it is more likely that the creature was imported directly from the Malayan jungle, being no more 'Manx' than the Sacred Cat of Burma is from Burma. However, there are many interesting stories of the origin of the Manx which conveniently ignore

*From *Lupercal*, by Ted Hughes, Faber and Faber.

history. Olivia Manning records that on the Isle of Man itself there is a story of a once upon a time when the Manx cat did have a tail, but the kits were so often stolen by the Irish soldiers (who used the tails as magical talismans on their shields) that the mother cats were reduced to biting off their kittens' tails to stop the useless slaughter.

All names are magical, or at least linked with magic, and so I may be forgiven for glancing at one or two names of wild cats which appeal to me. The Leopard Cat, for all its name, is little bigger than a domestic cat, and has a distinctive narrow muzzle, with a very short (distinctively ringed) tail, and two whitish stripes starting in the internal corners of the eyes, with similar streaks across the cheeks, as though it had donned warpaint in preparation for a hunt. Most of the species have dark spots, and it is this which brings the creature into a book on magic, for the Chinese call it the 'money cat', more poetically 'the precious metal cat' (*chin-ch'ien mao*), imagining that the numerous spots resemble their own money. One notes in the last of these three Chinese elements the onomatopoeic *mao* which means 'cat' and recalls the Mau of the Egyptian cult. Some delightful Chinese sayings concern the nature of the domestic cat. An action may be 'as dainty as a feeding cat'; false sympathy is 'the cat weeping for the rat'; but official collusion with criminals is 'the cat and the rat sleeping together'.

The Fishing Cat of the Orient is not afraid of water, and will wade into shallows or swim in search of its favourite diet of fish. The name came from the Bengali term *mach-bagral*, though for a very long time European naturalists believed that the cat did not like water at all. The Fishing Cat does more than fish, however. C. A. W. Guggisberg records the story of a missionary from the Malabar Coast who claimed that it would at times drag away small children for food. 'This story was met with a considerable amount of disbelief, but Sterndale once heard of a wild cat killed at Jeypore while in the act of carrying off a four-month-old infant. He thought that of all the felines smaller than a leopard only a fishing cat would have been capable of such a feat. The child, incidentally, was rescued alive.' Few cats like water, though tigers appear to delight in it and leopards are strong swimmers.

The name 'jaguar' for the *panthera onca* of the naturalists was long thought to come from the Tupi-Guarani language of the Amazonian regions, from the word *yaguara* which was imagined to mean 'wild beast that overcomes its prey with a bound'. However, it has recently been shown that the word *yagua* meant 'dog', making the original translation fanciful. Our modern word for the tiger has a much more respectable origin, however, for it is said that the name is from the old Persian *tighri*, which meant arrow. By the mediaeval period the word *tigrus* also meant striped – which just shows how the word-magic works: from the flight of an arrow, which also gave its name to the fast-flowing river Tigris, to a striped blanket in a thirteenth-century shop. The tiger came captive to Europe as a result of the invasions of Alexander the Great, and reached into Europe when one was made gift to the people of Athens by one of his generals. Less happy were those introduced to Rome at the beginning of our own era, for most of them fell victim to the gladiatorial games and animal hunt displays in the arenas. They were rare beasts even in the third century, yet the Emperor Elagabalus is said to have had over fifty killed in a single public display to celebrate his marriage, and to have used tigers to draw his triumphal chariot while he posed as Bacchus. This was what the Chinese would call 'treading on the tail of the tiger', and Elagabalus's vices and extravagances, of which the tiger incident was merely a part, resulted in his murder by the praetorian guards, who threw his mutilated body into the Tiber. The story of the vice-ridden Elagabalus's decline and fall has always satisfied me because he was rash enough to make a symbolic marriage to the Syrian Moon goddess Astarte, having her image transported from Carthage for the purpose. It is a foolish human who mocks the Moon goddess, and then mutilates her creatures.

Even the Emperor Nero had been wiser than Elagabalus, for he was so impressed by a tiger which fought valiantly in the arena that he named her Phoebe and had her placed in a golden cage in the gardens of his own Domus Aurea. Nero was of course well versed in magic: he knew full well that Phoebe was one of the names of the Moon, and he understood that a man teetering on the edge of sanity (as he was then) should propitiate with care the goddess who had rule over madness.

Among the most beautiful of all antique Roman mosaics is the series which were discovered in 1779 in the floor of the Emperor Hadrian's villa at Tivoli. One of these mosaic panels shows a battle between tigers, lions, panthers and centaurs. In the foreground a tiger is mauling a fallen centaur, but is shortly to be crushed to death by a rock which another centaur is about to throw on it. There is a rather delightful double meaning in the picture, for the centaur was the secret symbol of man's demonic and 'untamed' lower realm (of what we might nowadays call the unconscious), of that part which is distinctly bestial yet which he must carry with him wherever he goes. Here we see this wild and untamed part being attacked by the wild and untamed cats of the world.

When I first heard of the Pallas Cat I thought that here might lie an unexplored avenue into mythology, for Pallas was one of the titles of Athena, enshrined in the ancient mystery wisdom. What was so special about this wild cat that it should be linked by name with the esoteric tradition? Alas, the name has no such secret associations, for it is from Peter Simon Pallas, the eighteenth-century German naturalist who discovered the animal in Russia. I wonder about the magic of names, however, for the eyes of the Manul (as this cat is sometimes called) are big and directed outwards in that unblinking stare associated with the owl, and when one looks frontally at such a creature one might imagine it an owl grown legs. The point is that the attribute of Pallas Athena was an owl, and this became almost the symbol of the city to which she gave her name. Do names have a destiny, also – do names seek out creatures, rather than creatures seek out names?

The imagery attached to the nursery rhyme 'The Cat and the Fiddle' leaves little doubt that nowadays this word refers to the feline, and this notion has been carried well beyond the realm of nursery rhyme, for it has become a popular inn name and consequently an inn-sign. The juxtaposition is sometimes explained away in terms of the 'cat-gut' from which the fiddle strings are made, even though this gut has nothing to do with cats at all. But like so many themes connected with nursery rhymes, the cat and his fiddle do have a secret history, for we find several examples of cats playing fiddles in mediaeval church and cathedral symbols. Some suggest that the word 'fiddle' was a *double-entendre* in the secret language for *la fidèle*, French for 'the faithful'. A cat playing a fiddle could well be seen as a somewhat demonic image (the cat of the lunar Diana), indicating the way the satanic beast might use even the faithful as an instrument of his will. Of course, this ancient lore is now well hidden in the children's illustrations, though one cannot help noting how often the Moon itself appears in such images, as a sort of persistent reminder of the lost history of the names. Yet, persistent as the feline imagery is in modern times, it is unlikely that the cat was originally of the feline species. Some authorities have seen the cat of the church symbolism in quite a different light, suggesting that the word is an abbreviation for 'Catherine', one of the martyred saints. This would make the cat playing the fiddle a symbol for the *'fidèle Catherine'* who was faithful to

Christ even to the end.

In heraldry the cat family bears a curious selection of names which have become intimately bound up with word-sounds. In early heraldic texts the cat is termed a 'musion' and even a 'leyzard', but these words appear to have fallen out of favour. On heraldic devices and crests we find the tygre (as it is properly spelt in this arcane realm of symbolism), the cat, the wildcat, the civet and the 'cat of the mountains', which is often called the catamount. In heraldry, the lynx is portrayed with tufted ears and a short stump of a tail. In the heraldry of Britain probably the most famous cat crest is that of the City of Coventry (Plate 8), undoubtedly a cat in modern times but which appears in the past to have been a leopard. The curious Latin motto for this device means 'Chamber of the Prince', and is said to relate to the Black Prince who had a special association with the city in the fourteenth century. At a later point we shall reflect on the relationship between this Prince and the cat in his effigy at Canterbury (see Chapter 3).

According to some historians, the 'lions of England' were originally leopards, and the first king who definitely bore the three golden leopards on a red field was Richard I. We must be careful here, however, for we are already in the mire of heraldic obscurities, since in ancient heraldic forms a leopard (Leopart) was the technical name for a 'lion passant guardant'. In mediaeval texts we find that the leopard is a creature born of the mating of a lion (leo) with a pard, the name given to a panther which had no white specks on its coat.

'Three leopards of fine gold set in red; courant, fierce, haughty and cruel; to signify that like them the King is dreadful to his enemies, for his bite is slight to none who brave his anger . . .' says the armorial roll of 1300. It is likely that the first device to be adopted by an English king was the seal of a single lion, used by Henry I, which some have taken as a wise fulfilment of the prophecy recorded by Geoffrey of Monmouth, and made by the Arthurian wizard Merlin, that such a man would be 'a Lion of Justice'. There is a survival of this ancient magic in the 'leopard head' or 'King's Mark' found on some hallmarked silver: this, for all it often looks like the head of a cat, is really a lion's head.

A whole history of Europe is contained in the first quartering of this shield with that of France, which bore the fleur-de-lys on an azure field, which Edward III adopted in 1340. But, lion or leopard, the most occult element in this quartered shield is not the animal but the flower. The lily has an occult significance relating to the idea of birth, on the grounds that when the baby Hercules sucked at the breast of the goddess Hera, the milk which squirted out made the milky way of white stars in the heavens and the white lilies on the earth. However, some occultists insist that the stylized fleur-de-lys is not derived from the form of a lily, but from a bee. It is the same bee which is found on the statues of Diana of Ephesus, and carries us to the heart of hermetic symbolism. The bee has often been taken by occultists as a symbol of the human spirit dwelling in the physical body; some modern experts claim that this is because the internal temperature of the hive is the same as that of the human body. We see then an interesting esotericism in the quartering of the bee (or fleur-de-lys) with the lion or leopard, for the former has rule over the human heart. It is as though the device of Edward III put heart into the physical body of man, and these arms saw the glory of Agincourt and were carried by the Elizabethan seamen who broke the Spanish Armada. At all events, after the reign of Edward III England was destined to become the great nation of the future, taking precedence even over France. The lilies of the field had not been trampled, but gathered to make a new world from the old.

The arcane symbolism of the heraldic cat seems to be concerned more with the literary pun than with the limelight of history or the corridors of power, for the feline (not always a domestic cat) has been adopted as the crest or device of many families who have names sounding like 'cat'. For example, the demi-cat is a crest of the Keat family, as well as of the Cattley family. The tygre is favoured by the Keats, while Keate and Caterall have adopted the catamount passant. The Catesby have a leopard, the Catton two cats passant guardant. The Caton family 'of Binbrook' do not have a cat as their emblem but make a play on the word cat in their motto 'Cautus Metuit Foveam Lupus' (the cautious wolf fears the snare). There are many such punning mottoes and heraldic puns relating to the felines, as well as many mysteries, the cat-head on the memorial to Thomas Ferrers (Plate 9) being one of the most interesting.

Chapter Three

THE SACRED CAT IN LITERATURE

Hunting mice is his delight,
Hunting words I sit all night.

...

'Gainst the wall he sets his eye,
Full and fierce and sharp and sly;
'Gainst the wall of knowledge I
All my little wisdom try.

...

In our arts we find our bliss,
I have mine and he has his.

IRISH POEM *quoted by Helen Waddell*
in a translation by Robin Flower

It has been suggested that when Christianity supplanted the ancient religions, certain attributes of the Egyptian goddesses Isis, Bubastis and Sekhmet were incorporated into the imagery and associations of the Virgin Mary. This fact is expressed in the popular legend which tells that at the very same moment that Mary gave birth to Jesus in the stable, a mother cat also gave birth to a kitten. The legend is often symbolized in delightful paintings which show the Jesus child playing with a kitten. One of the most famous is the *Madonna of the Cat* by the sixteenth-century Urbanese painter Federico Baroccio, now in the National Gallery, London (figure 9), which depicts the young St John amusing Jesus by teasing a cat with a captive bird.

There may have been at least one secret strain of symbolism in this story, for certain beliefs about the cat widely held in those days, but nowadays dispensed with, throw some light on the 'Stable cat' story. For example, it appears to have been a superstition that the cat gave birth to its kittens from its mouth: perhaps this notion arose from the familiar sight of the cat carrying a kitten in its mouth, and no doubt the superstition was tinged more with humour than any sense of strict reality. However, there was also a belief in the antique world that the cat was impregnated by the ear. This notion is relevant to the 'Virgin cat' story, because it was widely believed that the Virgin Mary conceived Jesus through her ear, while listening to the Holy Spirit. Almost certainly the symbolism behind this curious belief is rooted in the idea of Christ as the Logos, the Word, issuing as it were from the mouth of God. Descending to the earth, the word is 'heard' by Mary, who conceives in this way. Some paintings and carvings depict this notion, more often than not by means of the dove (symbol of the Holy Spirit) pushing its beak into Mary's ear. Perhaps the parallels between the 'Stable cat' and the Virgin birth were more rooted in esotericism than is generally realized.

In earlier pictures (when such symbolism was more easily appreciated) it was a commonplace for artists to put a cross on the fur of the 'Jesus cat', to point to its Christian symbolism. However, there is a story in classical mythology which to some extent parallels the Christian legend, and may even have been the original source for it. As we all know, Apollo created the lion as his own solar creature, and so Diana, the Moon goddess, decided to create a smaller version, which was the cat. It may well be that this legend, benign as it is, was the origin of the later associations of evil bestowed upon the cat, for the lunar goddesses suffered a dark fate in Christian times, being merged with Hecate, the goddess of the Night.

The psychic powers of the cat are not always demonic (see Chapter 4, however), but like the demons who have feline heads, cats are said to be able to see the future and to be able to act upon their prevision. The most frequently quoted proof of this feline power of prediction is the story that when a cat deserts a house it is because it knows that a person living within that house will shortly die. In fact, the notion of an 'oracular cat' is very old. In Burma, there was Sinh, the cat with golden eyes, which was worshipped by a sect of priests who regarded it as having oracular powers. The Egyptian Bastet appears to have been called 'Mistress of the Oracle', while certain sacred cats were used for divinatory purposes in some Egyptian temples, although the true oracular cat of Egypt was actually a lion. The Sun-god Horus was represented in the form of a circular Sun flanked by two lions, the one to the left the lion of the past, that on the right the lion of the future. As we have seen, these pagan symbols, straight from the hermetic mystery wisdom, entered Christian art – in a form which has not been readily recognized by art historians – in the mediaeval pictures which depict lions or lions' heads on the armrests of the chair in which the Virgin Mary is seated. The conventional explanation of this symbolism is that the lions relate to the 'lion of Judah', but the correspondence with the Egyptian symbolism is more redolent with meaning, for it associates the Virgin and her Child with the solar power, with the 'Light' of St John's Gospel.

The Egyptian goddess Isis, on the other hand, was associated with the reflected light of the full Moon, and the connexion between the Egyptian cat and Isis is sufficiently well established for us to seek further links between the cat and the Virgin Mary, for the symbolism of the Christian Mother carries into our own culture many of the attributes of the Egyptian Isis, of which Bubastis and Sekhmet were aspects. Perhaps the most obvious connexion between Isis and Mary lies in the corn which is associated with both. Isis was one of the names of the ancient constellation Virgo, later associated with the Virgin Mary. This explains why both Isis and the Virgin Mother were sometimes called 'Mother of Corn' – though the esoteric symbolism is a little more complex than such simple-seeming names might suggest. There are many woodcuts and paintings which portray the Virgin Mother as a 'corn goddess', even to the extent of picturing her in a dress decorated with heads of corn. A more striking example is in the magnificent fifteenth-century triptych by Hugo van der Goes in the Uffizi, which depicts the Virgin adoring the child with a sheaf of corn on the floor below. It is in such paintings that we begin to sense the importance of the ancient words relating to corn, which often carried the idea of 'children' – for example the Assyrian word *bar* meant both 'corn' and 'son', and the ancient Babylonian Virgo of the stars carried the sheaf of corn which was also a child. The Latin word *spica* which denotes the corn in the hand of the stellar Virgo is in Greek the *stachys* which, besides meaning 'corn', also means 'offspring'. This stellar goddess was later associated with the son-bearing Virgin of Christian imagery, and it is in this light that the corn-dollies of rustic rituals must be seen. The occult symbolism surrounding the Christian Virgin Mother is replete with the triple meaning which turns the corn into a Son, and the Son into bread. All these associations are reflected not only in the making of corn-dollies, but also in the honouring of, even the sacrifice of, cats in the corn-harvesting festivals, for, as Oldfield Howey says:

> This Heavenly Corn, the Spica Virginis, the offspring of the Virgin, has like its early shadow, a Guardian Cat. The White Cat Moon, the Cleanser of the Night, or margaras who disperses the shadows by her silvery beams, is the Protector of the Celestial corn that the grey mice of night seek to devour and destroy. The milk-giving Virgin is the type of the Moon, and the cat is her ancient symbol.

In a deformation of this esoteric symbolism the mediaeval Church (which so easily forgot the ancient mysteries and symbols) associated the cat with the witch, herself a debased image of Isis and the Egyptian goddesses.

A curious, perhaps even horrific, merging of Christian and pagan 'Corn cat' lore may be seen in the ritual at Aix-en-Provence, originally conducted on Corpus Christi day, when a specially chosen tomcat was wrapped in swaddling clothes and treated like a holy child, adored and worshipped. The connexion with the pagan Sun-cults becomes evident at the moment the Sun passes the meridian, for the cat is then stripped of its clothing, placed in a wicker basket, and burned alive in the city square, to the (Christian!) singing of anthems. The magical element in the 'sacrificial god', and its links with the solar cult, point to an ancestry which is much older than Christianity, and raises the question as to how a domesticated cat (which did not exist in Europe in pagan times) should become the centre of the cult. Was it designed to merge the white and the black, the Christian and the demonic, into a single ritual of worship and purgation? Many of the partially Christianized cults and rituals of the Celts have been traced to Egyptian sources, which would suggest that at one time the Nordic Mystery Schools, of which the modern surviving Druidical schools are the superficial remnants, were in touch with the great secret Schools of Initiation in Egypt. How else might we explain such curious, yet well-established, facts as the Black Virgin cults, and this surprising survival of a solar cat?

It is an interesting reflection on the nature of the cat that while the domesticated cat was adopted by the Egyptians as a holy creature, and given special treatment, the cat was also regarded in Teutonic folk-lore as a companion of the gods. It is usually claimed, however, that the Egyptians declined to export their sacred smooth-haired cats and that the cat was not domesticated in northern Europe until fairly late. It follows that the cat which the Teutons selected as sacred to their goddess Freya, who was (as we might expect) a lunar queen, was almost certainly some sort of wild cat. Images of Freya in her chariot show her being drawn by two splendid lynxes. The goddess, whose name lingers still in our word Friday (Frigg's or Freya's Day), was a tutelary goddess of women, and her day used to be regarded as a good one on which to marry. Perhaps this was also connected with the harvest, and fecundity, over which she also had special rule.

Freya was demoted by the Christian Church into a demonic figure, reinforcing the Christian tradition of her namesake day, Friday (as the day on which Christ died), with the notion that it was favoured by witches for their awful sabbats. There are traces in accounts of cat-drawn Freya of the ancient lunar triplicities which we may note in the classical Diana, for one of her aspects was as Hel (sometimes 'Holda'), ruler of the dark underworld, and as 'Holle' she is goddess of domestic arts and therefore linked with the crafts of the earth. The triple nature is expressed exoterically in the nature of the cats who pull her chariot, for the cat is at once a goddess of the dark, of the sunlight and of the domestic hearth. The esoteric nature of the triple goddesses has been dealt with in an original way by Adam McLean, and it is clear that the threefoldness of the goddess, as indeed the threefoldness of the human being (which survives in a degenerate form in the classification of Intellect, Emotions and Body of the mediaeval occult system), is linked with the feline tradition. The cat-drawn Freya, and the Diana who emerged from the Egyptian Isis-tradition, was transformed into Artemis, to be associated later with the Virgin Maria, who still carried in her symbolism the image of the cat, are not the only triple goddess with the aspects of Heaven and Earth and Hell united in their one being.

The triple nature of Hecate, goddess of the black arts and an aspect of Diana Triformis, is clearly expressed in the classical imagery which gives her three bodies set back to back, enabling her to see in all directions. She is the dark mistress of the crossroads, which partly explains much of the later mediaeval mythology associated with her name. The fish which was left as an offering at the crossroads points to the feline connexion in a rather obvious way, but in a less obvious way so does the sacrifice of black puppies, for the dog is traditionally ruled by Mars, the masculine planet, while the cat is ruled by his spiritual opposite Venus, the feminine planet.

One of the great puzzles of cat-history is connected with the fact that the domesticated cat is supposed to have arrived in northern Europe as late as the eleventh or twelfth century, yet images of the cat, securely domesticated, are found in eighth- or ninth-century Celtic illuminations, and at the base of at least one important Celtic cross. This would suggest that the domesticated cat arrived in northern Europe much earlier than is generally believed. The smooth Egyptian cat came to Ireland, but like the new Christianity with which this 'white' cat came, he did not entirely supplant the darker cats of Irish legends which tell of the old ways, and of the old prowess of kings.

The marvellous mosaic of a cat which may still be seen in the remains of Roman Pompeii is clearly the image of a domestic cat. The destruction (or preservation) of Pompeii by the volcanic lava flow of AD 96 occurred at a time when it is possible that Christians were already active in that city, and so it is not too imaginative for us to trace a direct lineage from this mosaic cat to the Christian felines which we find in the early Christian art of Ireland. It is likely indeed that the domestic cat was imported by the monks who travelled northwards to establish their monastic systems in the British Isles from the late fourth century onwards. This

Fig. 13   Enlarged detail of cats with rats or mice from the 'Chi-Rho' page of the Book of Kells. Trinity College Library, Dublin

would explain why the thoroughly Christian image of cats sitting peacefully among a bevy of rats or mice (figure 13) may be seen in one of the fascinating details of the monogram page of the Book of Kells, which was painted in that Irish monastery in the eighth century. The enlargement in figure 13 indicates why this page has been described as 'the most elaborate specimen of calligraphy which was perhaps ever executed'.

The peaceable cats are not merely decoration, for this tiny detail, like all the others on this page, is intended to symbolize something relating to the Christian faith. The rats are nibbling the Eucharistic bread which should be used in the Mass, and it has been suggested that this is an allusion to 'unworthy receivers', to those who are in sin yet choose to take the body of Christ. The cats, therefore, would be symbols of the final judgement which awaits such people. Are these cats demonic, then? We hardly think so, for had the scribe wished to portray them as minions of the Devil, he would have given them ghastly features, or at least indicated something of their demonic nature. Whoever painted these guardian cats was a lover of the feline race, and obviously well versed in their nature. A different view of the symbolism of the detail sees the two traditional enemies in harmony: a way of expressing the notion that when the Christian message is rightly understood, even the lion and the lamb will lie together in peace.

There is a series of related 'Christian' cats at the base of the Muireadach Celtic cross of Monasterboice (County Louth) in Ireland. One of these appears to be licking a newly born kitten, while the other is teasing or eating a captured bird (figure 14). They sit almost as guardians over the dedication panel, which reads in Irish *Or do Muireadach las ndearnad in Chros*, 'A prayer for Muireadach who caused this cross to be made'. This Muireadach was Abbot of Mainistir Buithe (St Buith's Abbey) until 922, which is again somewhat early for images of domestic cats in this northern place. As has been mentioned, at one time it was a practice of Christian artists to put a cross on the back of cats intended to recall those born in the stable at the same time as Christ, so we may see in these cats almost a humorous symbolism, for they carry above the socle upon which they are carved an enormous seventeen-foot-high monolithic cross.

Another early mediaeval cat of monastic fame is a literary one, quoted in part at the head of this chapter – this being a feline companion in the song sung by an eighth-century scholar in the monastery of St Paul in

Fig. 14   Two cats with rat and bird – detail of the base of the Monasterboice Cross in the County Louth. Lithograph from H. O'Neill's The Sculptured Crosses of Ancient Ireland, *1853*

Carinthia, Austria, and yet another sign that the cat was domestic in those monastic cells. The scholar's cat is called Pangur Bán, an Irish name if ever there was one. The symbolism is delightful, and is yet another confutation of the notion that the domesticated cat came to Europe late in the tenth or early in the eleventh century. I like to think that those monks who carried bags of earth across the waves to that last rock bastion of the Skelligs in County Kerry (the point furthest west in Europe) in order to make gardens in the small cavities of the rock faces, also carried kittens in their bags. I have spent nights alone in the remains of the monastery there, and know that the monks would need companionship in the teeth of the wind's loneliness.

However, Ireland did have its darker cats before the monks sought refuge in that land, as we witness in accounts of the cat of Finn. The cat in the Irish fairy tales is scarcely Christian, and to judge from the Rackham illustration (Plate 10) is not domesticated. The old tales tell of Iruscan, the King of the Cats, who was as big as an ox and lived in a cave at Knowth in Meath. The poet Senchan who sang at the feast given by Marban was unwise to satirize both mice and cats, the latter because they permitted the mice to run free enough to get their whiskers into his eggs. The tale tells how Iruscan is angry at the satire, and carries off Senchan to devour him, but St Ciaran saves the poet by hurling a red-hot bar at the cat, thereby killing it.

The defeat of a local demon by Christian saints is not a story told by the old singers: it must be a tale adapted or imported by Christians. The power of the old cat could not be allayed by hot iron, as the more pagan tales insist. Folklore is in awe of this Iruscan, and tells how an Irish countryman killed an ordinary cat. Before it died the victim said, 'Go home, and boast to your wife how you killed the King of the Cats.' Now the cat in truth was no king, but he was wiser than the countryman, for as soon as he was back in his home he told his wife that he had killed the King of the Cats. In one bound the domesticated house cat, until then lying idly by the fire, leapt up and tore out the man's throat, as the only possible punishment for such a deed.

Stories of cat lore abound in Christian contexts, but the one I like most of all is that about the eccentric Reverend Hawker of Morwenstow. Hawker is now chiefly remembered for the curious chimneys on the vicarage which he designed to serve his Cornwall church, but, in the words of the historian Michael Williams, he was 'a legend in his lifetime'. Hawker is said to have invited nine cats into his service, then excommunicated one because it caught a mouse on Sunday.

Many of the more beautiful Oriental cats were regarded as being sacred. Some few Siamese cats have what is called 'the Temple Mark' just a little lower down than the back neck, giving the impression that someone with dirty hands has lifted the cat in his fingers. The Siamese priests consider such cats to be particularly sacred, and tell the story of how the first temple mark was made when a god picked up the cat, leaving the shadow of his fingers on the cat's descendants. In an article in *Cat Gossip* Dr Lilian Veley describes another eastern sacred cat in Japanese literature and social life, which is believed to be the 'house' of a distinguished ancestor. An example, which was stolen for filthy lucre from a Japanese temple, was brought back to England, and its black 'sacred' mark was photographed several times. This was said by the imaginative to resemble a woman in a kimono.

Outside the Christian context it is rare for the cat of mediaeval literature or art to be symbol of anything other than the 'demonic', or of what the thirteenth-century scholar Nackam called 'the full lecherous beast'. However, at the very end of the mediaeval era this feline symbolism was to change, if only for a short while. When the poet Langland revised his popular fable, *The Vision Concerning Piers Plowman* in 1377, he tells of a cat which frightens the mice:

> For a cat of a courte · came when hym lyked,
> And oerlepe hem lyztlich · and lauzte hem at his wille,
> And pleyde with hem perilouslych · and possed hem aboute.

The symbolism is thinly disguised political satire. As Francis Klingender points out in his entertaining *Animals in Art and Thought*, Langland's revisions were intended to reflect the tense political atmosphere in England at the time. The 'cat of a courte' is unequivocally symbol of King Edward III, and the kitten which would follow the cat and persecute the mice was his grandson, heir to the throne and future Richard II. When Langland made these revisions, Edward was clearly in his declining years (indeed, he died in that same year), and the kingdom was already under the repression of John of Gaunt. Of course, such symbolism is still tinged with the 'demonic' quality with which the cat had been invested, for the mice (the people of England) feared both cat and kitten, like the mice in Langland's fable, who decided that it was pointless trying to tie a bell around the cat's neck when, like as not, the kitten would be just as bad as the cat.

The demonic associations of the kitten, which the mice imagined would 'cracchy us and all owre kynde', might be linked with the fact that his father was the Black Prince. In popular thought the epithet 'black' is often considered to arise from either the prince's moral disposition or the colour of his armour, though in fact it is more likely to be derived from the sable of his heraldic device and to have nothing to do with the dark forces. However, it is quite possible that the laughing feline face of the heraldic lion which figures on the effigy-armour of the Black Prince in Canterbury Cathedral is linked with the feline symbolism of the poem, the hunting 'cat of courte' being the debased lion of England.

Mediaeval symbolism often worked on a multi-layer principle incorporating divergent nuances which is quite foreign to modern methods of symbolization. The symbols on the thirteenth-century sketchbook page of Villard de Honnecourt in figure 15 reflect this. The cat at the top of the page looks distinctly demonic, while the cat at the bottom left is merely a domestic cat cleaning itself. Even so, we cannot avoid observing that this latter cat is twisting into a position which is almost in imitation of

Fig. 15 Cat, among such creatures as grasshopper, fly, crayfish, etc. and a maze of the kind still set in the marble floor of Chartres Cathedral. Page from the sketchbook of Villard de Honnecourt. Bibliotheque Nationale, Paris

the adjacent drawing of the 'maze'. This drawing is very close to the so-called labyrinth in Chartres Cathedral, and to surviving 'mazes' in mediaeval churches throughout Europe, yet it is not really a maze or a labyrinth at all, for it is quite impossible to lose oneself in its convolutions. There is no doubt that it is actually a ritual dance pattern, as much linked with the initiation lore of the time as the grasshopper in the top

left of de Honnecourt's drawings. The purpose of the maze was to conduct the pilgrim towards the centre – towards that still point of the dance
where the peace of Christ would be found. Is it possible that the cat, in
imitating this circular movement, is symbolically dancing and striving
for this inner peace? Could this de Honnecourt cat be a symbol of the
Virgin, a throwback to the original significance of the cat as Queen of the
Night?

The cat offered many potentials as a symbol in both political satire
and moral literature, but the witchcraft craze in the latter parts of the
mediaeval period scotched almost all the non-demonic layers. This
realm of feline demonism is examined in Chapter 6, but it accounts for
the relative hiatus in cat-symbolism (other than the demonic) until the
seventeenth and eighteenth centuries, when the English artist Hogarth
eventually succeeded in liberating the cat from its demonic associations,
and carrying it into the literary journalism for which his engravings are
famous (see Chapter 5).

The 'political' cat symbolism of George Wither in his collection of
emblems is nevertheless of the same genre as that used by Langland,
though since it is intended as a general political satire it reflects on a less
royal, yet no less insidious, corruption and evil. In the relevant engraved
roundel (figure 16) Wither shows the cat itself caged, with mice playing
fearlessly around. The scene, he tells us, shows that

> When Magistrates confined are,
> They revell, who were kept in feare.

This cat fitly represents a 'Tyrannous, or wicked Magistrate', for though
the mice be a harmful vermin, and the cat their remedy, yet even so

> A ravenous Cat, will punish in the Mouse,
> The very same Offences, in the house,
> Which hee himselfe commits; yea, for that Vice,
> Which was his owne (with praise) he kils the Mice;
> And, spoyleth not anothers life alone,
> Ev'n for that very fault which was his owne.
> But feeds, and fattens, in the spoyle of them.
> ...
> More torturing them, 'twixt fruitlesse hopes and feares,
> Than when their bowels, with his teeth he teares:
> For, by such terrour, and much crueltie,
> Hee kills them, ten times over, e're they die.

Half way up Highgate Hill, from which there used to be an excellent view over London, is the bronze model of a cat, marking the spot where Dick Whittington and his feline companion stopped to rest while leaving the city and were persuaded back by the promise in the sound of the bells. The story of Dick's 'return', and indeed the whole account of the role played by his cat in the story of his becoming Lord Mayor of London, is almost certainly fictitious, though there was a Richard Whittington who was first sheriff and then Mayor of London several times between 1397 and 1419. Indeed, in 1416 he was elected Member of Parliament for London.

The cat, however, is more elusive than the master, and we must ask how this fictitious cat entered into the English mythology, and why it has become so important that the cat of the Whittington pantomime is nowadays more firmly fixed in the hearts of most children than Dick himself. The historical Richard Whittington apparently did walk to London, and did marry his master's daughter, and even prospered until he was an exceedingly wealthy man, but a cat plays little or no part in the true history. Was it, like the Italo-French counterpart Puss in Boots, a

Fig. 16   Caged cat illustrating 'When Magistrates confined are, They revell, who were kept in feare'. From George Wither's A Collection of Emblems, Ancient and Moderne, 1635 edition

Fig. 17 *'Foss Passant'. Drawing by Edward Lear of his pet cat, Foss*

relic of hermetic and occult symbolism?

The academic answer is dry as dust. It has been pointed out that since Whittington rose to power through purchase or bribery, and that such profitable enterprise was in those days called 'achat' (though French, it was seemingly pronounced in those times with a hard c, to give the sound 'acat') the confusion between 'acat' and 'a cat' is understandable in later expansions of the rags-to-riches story. Other explanations have been offered, but few historians believe that a feline was involved in Whittington's translation to the Mayoralty of London. In academic terms, the model of the cat which sits securely within the railings on Highgate Hill (Plate 11) is a symbol of that great myth-maker which we call false etymology.

It is a relief to turn away from the lost symbolism of Whittington's imaginary cat to the real cats of Edward Lear, and especially to his own cat Foss, who lived a zany life with the artist for seventeen years, and had the good fortune to be buried in Italy, in the garden of his master's villa at San Remo. But what has Lear's cat, caught in a few brilliant lines of a master draughtsman (figure 7), to do with arcane symbolism? The answer is probably nothing at all, for Lear immortalized his friend without secret devices – his 'Foss, Passant' in the gallery of the cat's heraldic blazons (figure 17) is probably one of the most famous drawings of a cat to have survived from the nineteenth century. Yet Lear was too superb a master of pun and arcane literary joking not to put such jokes into his drawings, and we may be sure that if we regard all his drawings and poems as being merely 'Nonsense', we shall miss half the fun. Is there a symbolic meaning in the seeming-nonsense poem 'The Owl and the Pussycat'? These two went to sea in a beautiful pea-green boat, and after a few diversions were married by a turkey who lives on the hill (figure 18).

> And hand in hand, on the edge of the sand,
> They danced by the light of the moon,
>   The moon,
>   The moon,
> They danced by the light of the moon.

The reference to the Moon itself might start the occultist looking more deeply into the meaning of this 'nonsense' poem, especially when he notes that in the first few lines the owl 'looked up to the stars above'. In fact, one of the most abiding symbols of the Moon is that used as a sacred emblem by the Ottoman Turks. The reason why this symbol was adopted are complex, but it appears to have been first used in the thirteenth century by the Sultan of Iconium from Byzantium (later Istanbul): it was eventually taken for the Turkish flag, along with its star. Whatever the history of this lunar symbolism, we find in Lear's poem a reference to the stars, the Moon, and to a turkey.

Fig. 18 The cat who married the owl. Drawing by Edward Lear to illustrate his poem 'The Owl and the Pussy-cat', from the 1871 edition of his Nonsense Songs

The owl is of course the traditional symbol of the Greek goddess Athena (and later of the Roman equivalent Minerva). In Christian symbolism the owl is widely seen as a bird of the night, concerned with hidden wisdom and with the secret tradition. One wonders, indeed, if the inner content of the poem has anything to do with the fact that it was written in the year the declaration of Papal infallibility was pronounced?

We should realize by now that it is virtually impossible to give an explanation of the cat's hidden symbolism in a few words, for the cat of history and symbolism is as elusive as the living cat itself. However, we may be sure that for Lear the cat was a symbol of joy and life, the creature of the spirit. In his first illustration to the poem, the cat steers the boat on the waters as they set out on their adventure – she knows the secrets of navigation, while the owl merely lies back and serenades her with a guitar. The cat and the owl are both creatures of the night, while the turkey is symbol of a pagan country. Is the marriage between a cat and an owl beneath the light of the Moon a thinly disguised commentary on the joys of lunar 'paganism', which unites the life forces of the cat with the hidden wisdom of the owl?

Perrault, with his 'Master Cat', which appeared in his 1697 edition of *Tales of Mother Goose*, did much to redeem the diabolical image of the cat, for on superficial acquaintance his story of Puss in Boots is not overtly arcane, and does not appear to moralize. The cat is received as a bequest by the son of a recently deceased miller. The son is not too happy at the gift, for his brothers have received far more valuable presents of a mill and an ass – both far superior to a cat. The gift turns out to be more than a standard domestic cat, however, for the puss can talk. He tells the boy not to worry – his gift is far, far better than those left to his brothers, as he shall see. First, however, the boy must have some boots made for the cat. These boots are important, and have entered into the stream of popular mythology in many images which portray the cat virtually in the guise of a cavalier (figure 19).

By a series of stratagems this strangely booted cat first lures a rabbit into a bag and then persuades the King that his master is the Marquis of Carabas, a wealthy landowner, and induces the King to make over a gift of new clothing suitable to this rank. In order to provide a suitable home for his master, the enterprising Puss persuades an ogre (who conveniently lives in a magnificent castle) to change into a mouse, and then gobbles him up. By this stratagem, the castle becomes the domain of the new Marquis, whose wealth so impresses the King that he gives his daughter's hand in marriage to the erstwhile miller's son.

Perrault tries not to point a moral. The cat, like his owner, becomes a great lord, and that is sufficient reward. It is an arcane fairy story, but its meaning has often been missed by those who fail to understand that most of the old fairytales contain a secret wisdom. George Cruikshank saw the tale as little more than a series of lessons in the success of falsehoods, and for his own edition of the fairy story (1870) reworked the ending, turning the cat into a man. While it would seem to me to matter little whether a cat or a man tells lies, the transformation does provide a moral, even if this has nothing to do with Perrault's tale. Cruikshank has his booted cat announce that he is really the former gamekeeper of the true Marquis of Carabas, and had been changed into a cat for not being sufficiently appreciative of his fortune in being human. Here we have the moral, perhaps pointed just a little obtusely, with none of Perrault's grace. Cruikshank's meddling is a good example of how a little understanding can lead one to miss the whole point of an arcane symbolism.

The English title of the story when it appeared in the 1729 *Histories, or Tales of Past Times* was 'The Master Cat, or Puss in Boots'. The image passed into generations of popular fairytales in which the cat, booted or otherwise, was the subtle hero of a thousand escapades. Who was this superior cat, and why did he wear boots? He wears boots on the flimsiest of excuses: at the very beginning of the tale, after revealing to his new master that he can speak, he demands that his master have a pair of boots made for him, so that he can go through the undergrowth. What is the secret symbolism of these boots, which degenerated into symbols to hang outside French cobbler shops to designate the trade practised inside?

We have already noted that this cat is not quite what he seems to be, and that his symbolism is involved with the arcane realms. The significance of the boots in this story obviously depends upon the significance of the cat. What is the Puss? Well, he is first and foremost a gift from the boy's father, an hereditary gift. The first obvious absurdity is the notion that a puss should wear boots. This is itself a deep symbolism. What cat needs to have its paws protected from the undergrowth? Puss has to be specially protected from the world – the rough undergrowth is not his proper realm. The boots therefore symbolize the fact that Puss is not a cat of this world, but needs special protection. The cat is really a symbol of man's inner vision, a delicate and spiritual thing which can all too easily be ripped and torn in the undergrowth of the world. The cat has the vision to see the worth of the rabbit, the importance of the King to his master, the value of the ogre, and the need for his master to marry the King's daughter.

It need not concern us here that the King and the King's daughter are

Fig. 19 Puss in Boots. A wood engraving after Dore's drawing to illustrate Perrault's fairy tales. Puss has hidden the clothes of his master, who is bathing in the river. The king is passing by, so Puss calls out lustily that some thief has run off with the garments of the Marquis of Carabas. The king supplies the supposed nobleman with a magnificent suit from his own wardrobe, marking the beginning of the puss-owner's rise to fortune

standard symbols from alchemy, pointing to the innermost nature of man's being. We need only note that the marriage represents the fulfilment of all the boy's aims – yet he himself, without the aid of his cat, could neither see these aims nor devise a way to attain them.

The ogre and his castle are the darker elements which may be found in all men. The ogre is that dark guardian of many fairytales, who must be tricked, bypassed or transformed, for he is the unseeing and unseen darkness in all men. His castle is a dark realm which must be explored or put to a better use: usually in such a castle there is a treasure for the hero to find. The booted cat is astute enough to have the ogre transformed conveniently into the shape of a mouse. Once again, it is not the boy who can escape or use the ogre, but his inner vision, his cat, who has that power. It is also the cat who sees how the castle of the giant may be used – to further impress the King. Is it merely accident that there is already a sumptuous meal spread in this castle, so that the King, the boy and his princess may dine in splendour? The castle did not really belong to the ogre, no more than did his treasures – it was the boy's all along, just as was the hand of the beautiful princess his rightful claim – yet only the cat had the wisdom to see this.

The symbolism of this Master Cat is extraordinary, and shows how profoundly a writer may change the image of a creature, which even in 1697 was still branded as the witch's familiar, when working it into the structure of an esoteric tale.

Perrault did not invent the story; he merely wove together several strands from older tales in which the cat helped his master, in much the same way as a London cat was supposed to help his Whittington. Another seventeenth-century version of the story provides a different ending quite worthy of Perrault, if less happy. In this, the newly married boy and princess swear eternal gratitude to the cat. After Puss dies, they will have his body preserved and placed in a golden cage. But the cat knows better than to trust in human words, and is too clever for them. Puss feigns death. Much as the cat had expected, his master forgets his promises, and is on the point of throwing the body from a castle window. Puss in Boots stands up and castigates the lack of gratitude, and then leaves the boy, the castle and the princess to their own devices. The price of the boy's ingratitude is the loss of his invaluable inner vision.

With Puss in Boots the symbolism of the cat is being refined, returned as it were to the esoteric meaning of the ancient Egyptians. The earliest interpreters showed the cat as symbol of human vision – a symbolism not unconnected with the fabled power of the cat's eyes which may see even in the dark. But now we have a French writer showing the cat as symbol of the inner vision, a cat who needs to be protected from the outer world, but which has the power to see in space and time.

The Cheshire cat which Alice encountered during her journey through Wonderland has the most famous grin in English literature. Neither cat nor grin has been adequately explained, yet it is clear that there are many esoteric references within the text, and we may be sure that Lewis Carroll had some interesting symbolism in mind. So subtle are many of his arcane references in both the text and the illustrations (drawn for the wood-block cutter according to Carroll's very precise instructions by Tenniel – that the general reader may be forgiven for missing them, no matter how many times he reads the adventure story.

The engraving by Tenniel which shows Alice holding the 'baby' which has been transformed into a piglet (figure 20) contains a most interesting example of this sort of hidden personal symbolism, to which Martin Gardner refers in his *The Annotated Alice*. Carroll himself had pointed out that the foxglove in the background to the 'piglet' drawing of figure 20 had a meaning, since, as he points out in all earnestness, foxes do not wear gloves (no more than babies turn into piglets, one supposes). The origin of the word 'foxgloves' is 'folks-gloves', says Carroll, who then reminds his reader that one of the names for fairies was the 'good folk'. This kind of literary punning is the very essence of his *Alice in Wonderland*, and we should not be surprised to find that the Cheshire cat is linked with a similar personal play on the arcane.

In fact, the 'piglet' drawing and the Cheshire cat are related in a very special way. When Lewis Carroll invented what he called 'The Wonderland Postage-Stamp Case', he designed it so that no one would be able to sell a similar one in the shops. His own appears to have been bought from a firm in Oxford, and was really a cardboard case of a very simple design intended to hold postage stamps. The case itself was held in an envelope-like cover, on which was printed a picture of Alice holding the Duchess's baby. However, when the inside case was drawn out, there was printed on this the transformation of the baby into the piglet and the Cheshire Cat smiling its inane pre-vanishing grin. Carroll explained that he had used these pictures because, although imitations would surely appear, these could not 'include the two Pictorial Surprises, which are copyright'. In fact, this transformation meant that the human (baby) was revealed as being both subhuman (the piglet) and godlike (the cat).

Fig. 20   Alice nursing the piglet. Wood engraving after Tenniel's illustration to Alice in Wonderland

Carroll was too fond of such double meanings for this symbolism not to have been intentional as well as 'copyright'.

Carroll's joking and punning may be almost schoolboyish, yet several interesting notions are expressed in the idea of a vanishing cat. First of all, let us note that he is making use of the ancient link between the Cat and the Moon, which is possibly why the feline is depicted high on a tree, against the sky. When the cat disappears, it leaves only a crescent of teeth behind, and even the very word 'crescent' evokes the Moon which, as everyone knows, is made of cheese. 'Cheese' is in turn the very word which the photographer has us say when he wishes to record our smile or grin. This may seem a slight explanation of the grinning cat, yet we should remember that Carroll was an enthusiastic and indeed very proficient photographer.

Then again, the almost symbolic wood engraving which shows the Cheshire cat looking down in fiendish amusement at the arguing cards (figure 1) is not without its arcane significance. The executioner has been ordered by the mad Queen to cut off the head of the Cheshire cat, but he argues with perfectly good logic that he cannot cut off the head of something which has no body. The King counters that anything with a head can be beheaded. The point is that in the illustration the body-free cat is peering down as they argue about the relationship between head and body. Just as the card bodies of the playing cards (the 'court' cards, to mention just another pun) are unreal, so is the body of the cat – and even its head is capable of disappearing, leaving behind only its grin. After all, everything that happened in Wonderland (and perhaps everything which happens in our own world) is really only so much 'moonshine'. The Cheshire cat's head appears something like a full Moon, hovering over the illusory cardboard world below.

Perhaps the name Cheshire is merely a reference to Cheshire cheese, and therefore to the smile or grin, but it could be that there is a more arcane symbolism in Carroll's choice of the word. Cheshire, where Carroll spent his early years, was a County Palatine, the dominion of an earl palatine in which the count had royal privileges. Ebenezer Brewer records one tradition which tells that the cats in Cheshire are perpetually laughing because the idea of a County Palatine is so absurd. A Duchess is the wife or widow of a Duke, and thus the Duchess whom Alice encountered was of higher rank than an Earl palatine, which is perhaps why she is so dismissive of the cat when Alice asks her about it. We must recall that it is the Duchess who tells Alice that it is a 'Cheshire Cat'. It has been observed that Cheshire cheeses were once moulded in the shape of a grinning cat – yet this should not disguise the essentially arcane symbolism in the story. In her psychoanalytical analysis of Carroll, Phyllis Greenacre points out that at one level of meaning is the fantasy that the cheesy cat may eat the rat that would eat the cheese. But there is no rat mentioned in the text, and it might be better to see in the Cheshire cat the humour of its being a lunar symbol, derived from the Egyptian Bastet mythology, with a lunar face which laughs, like the man in the Moon, and a crescent grin. The Cheshire cat waxes and wanes, appears and disappears just like the Moon itself. Such an interpretation will explain why the Duchess and Alice discuss whether it would be advantageous to speed up time.

Some writers have suggested that the grinning cat was inspired by the laughing head carved on the south transept arch of Cranleigh parish church, Surrey. While we do sometimes find feline creatures in English church architecture (see, for example, page 175), there is no evidence to suggest that the Cranleigh carving is intended to represent a cat at all – indeed, it is merely a standard grinning demon-face, the like of which is found in several late mediaeval churches. Far better, and certainly more feline, heads are found on the south door of Iffley Church, near Oxford.

In fact, one does not have to go to Cranleigh in search of feline laughing grotesques. The church in Daresbury, where Carroll lived as a boy, has on the north side a number of leonine grinning gargoyles which could well have suggested the idea of a grinning cat to a sensitive boy. Daresbury parish church is worth a visit for many reasons, not least of which is the splendid memorial stained glass in the east end which portrays the main creatures of Wonderland – including, of course, the grinning disembodied cat.

The distance between the Cheshire Cat and the lion Aslan of Narnia in the modern stories for children, is not so great as one might imagine, though the Cheshire Cat is distinctly pagan in comparison with the Christian symbolism favoured by C. S. Lewis. Lewis's allegorical Narnia series is steeped in Christian esotericism because Lewis was innately interested in such strains of secret symbolism, and in many realms of thought which may nowadays be called occult. Ginger, the cat of *The Last Battle* (in which book the untame lion Aslan dissolves the outer shell of Narnia), is bathed in symbolism of a thinly disguised mediaeval quality. Before the terrible evil is unleashed in Narnia, this cat is 'a great big Tom in the prime of life', who sits bolt upright with the tail curled around his toes in the very front of all the Beasts. Being a cat, he is both street-wise and astute, and appears to be first among the animals to see that the Narnians are being conned by the awful Ape Shift. However, Ginger's instinctively evil nature encourages him to collude with the ape, as a result of which he achieves dubious fame as the first of the talking animals to revert to his 'natural state' as a dumb animal.

The fate of this ginger tom is the first evidence of the promise made by Aslan 'at the beginning of the world' when he turned the beasts of Narnia into Talking Beasts and 'warned them that if they weren't good they might one day be turned back again and be like the poor witless animals one meets in other countries'. The delightful illustrations by

Pauline Baynes could not offer a more telling contrast between the suspicious cat seated among the newly puzzled Talking Beasts (figure 21) and the terrified moggy which, in its superman flight of terror back through the doorway, knocks over the Ape Shift. He is of course fleeing from his sight of the demon king, the opposite power to Aslan, whom the evil Calormenes called Tash – an infernal personage straight from a mediaeval grimoire or demon book, with the head of a bird and four arms, moving over the grass as though floating, the grass withering beneath him as he goes.

Part of the force of the allegory is that when each animal or human passes through the doorway of the hut it sees the world it deserves, as a reflection of its own inner life. The doorway is indeed an occult symbol, the passage from ordinary life to that higher life which men call death, guarded by what modern occultists term the 'Guardian of the Thresh-

Fig. 21   The talking animals puzzling about what the ape has said. Illustration by Pauline Baynes to C. S. Lewis's **The Last Battle,** *the final book in the 'Narnia' series. Reproduced with the permission of the publishers, William Collins, from the 1985 edition*

old', which is a part of their own dark self. The dark self which the cat sees must be terrifying, for it reduces him from a self-confident Talking Animal back into a wild cat: 'The Cat was trying to say something, but nothing came out of his mouth except the ordinary, ugly cat-noises you might hear from any angry or frightened Tom . . .' Within the C. S. Lewis allegory, the cat therefore retains the demonic element, precisely as the demon king Tash preserved the characteristics of demons described and pictured in mediaeval grimoires. He is, in a sense, the familiar of the ape, who is in turn proved to be nothing more than a puppet of the evil Calormenes, who (in turn) are merely the vassals of the demon Tash.

We are so accustomed to treating Aesop's fables as 'moral tales' (which they undoubtedly are) that we tend to ignore the fact that many occultists claim that they are really arcane stories. A fine example, in which the cat symbolism reflects the human state, is the fable which tells of the eagle, sow and cat who live in the same tree. The eagle builds his nest at the top of the tree, the wild sow and her young live at the foot of the tree, while the cat and her family occupy a hollow in the trunk half way down. The three live in some harmony until the cat exercises its evil nature, and tells the eagle to beware the sow, which is intending to uproot the tree by grubbing away among its roots. The eagle is terrified, so then the cat climbs down the trunk and tells the sow to beware the eagle, which is surely awaiting a good moment to swoop down and carry off its young piglets as food. The eagle and the sow are by now so alarmed that they stay in their respective places, not even venturing out to obtain food for their families, as a result of which they all starve. Their bodies supply the cat with ample nourishment for her hungry litter.

The story has several morals, of course, perhaps the main being that we should not believe all we hear. However, the fable may also be seen within an arcane context as relating to the human being, and to what are sometimes called the 'three parts of man'. Most of the old fairy stories which centre around trees or tree-trunks are about the secret nature of man, for the trunk is one of the arcane symbols of man's spine, the roots of which are gathered in the brain as symbol of the way man is himself rooted in the invisible spiritual world. Many occult images portray the tree as an image of man; perhaps the most famous is that diagram which summarizes so perfectly the cosmic order of the cabbalists, which is usually called the 'Sephirothic Tree'. For the cabbalist the upper is reflected in the lower, so the upper cosmic realm is visualized in the form of a tree spread out in space and time, while the lower realm (which is man) is also visualized as a tree, with the roots encased in the brain and the branches stretching down into the lower world. The brain, the source of the spiritual life, is thus the fount of man's life.

What are these three creatures which live in the spinal tree of Aesop? The eagle is a symbol of human thinking, which like man's conceiving may soar into the heavens. The cat is symbol of the human emotional life, while the sow is symbol of man's physical being, of his will-life, which operates in the lower regions: it has not the intellectual brilliance of the eagle, and none of the sensitive street-wise cleverness of the cat.

As we have seen from this glance at the esoteric cat, the roots of the symbolism which may be traced in European literature have had a rich soil to nourish them. The cat is at once a symbol of wisdom, yet (as Lewis's Narnia tale so well represents) it is a wisdom derived from an acuity of vision which may be dulled as the creature is pulled into the mire. The everlasting cat has its dark shadow, and the shade of wisdom is vacuity. The tradition of feline symbolism within occult contexts reflects this duality between wisdom and vacuity, so that the cat is at one moment as worldly-wise as that which helped Perrault's hero, at another as vacuous and ephemeral as the Cheshire Cat. Yet the truth of the matter is that, seen within the occult context, this very duality is an important aspect of feline symbolism; for the cat really represents the human being, that biped dualism who contains within himself all things, from the fruits of esoteric wisdom to the vacuity of selfish inanity. It is this deep level of symbolism which the cat touches to perfection, for there is in literature, as in art, the Christian cat with the cross marked in its fur, and the demonic cat with the light of Hell in its eyes. It is a duality which stretches across the entire world, yet is united in this single symbol of the cat, for in truth the esoteric cat is the human being, itself a being of the stars who is temporarily knee-deep in the mud, wearing heavy boots which keep him on the earth, literally a *chat botté*.

It is interesting that when we study the cat in religious symbolism, we see little more than the degeneration of a feline goddess into the lower ranks of demons or into the frightful symbolism of the cat-familiar of witches. However, when we pursue the secret symbolism of the cat in non-theological literature we are not drawn downwards into the infernal realms with the same urgency or lack of grace: we are led rather to examine the inner nature of the cat. This pathway of literature leads us into a portrayal of what has been called in modern times the 'psychic cat' (see chapter 4), which certainly has some dealings with the dark occult realm of spirits, ghosts and even demons, but which is essentially a representative of the psychic soul of man, of the human unconscious, the gradual education of which will reveal the whole future of humanity. This psychic cat, which belongs purely to neither the higher world nor the lower, is the one who chooses to live half way up (or down) the tree, where she acts as a sort of guardian between the roots (which reach into hell) and the branches (which reach into heaven).

Chapter Four

THE PSYCHIC CAT

The archetypal cat knows its way about our inner world,
and can direct us to treasures lying hidden in the recess of
our minds.

PATRICIA DALE-GREEN,
The Cult of the Cat

Towards the end of his life, the Victorian poet Matthew Arnold wrote an
elegiac poem on the death of his canary, Matthias. In the poem he mentions with some reverence his deceased pet cat Atossa, who, in her old
age, would lie beside the canary's cage, eyeing the bird 'with a soul
resign'd'. The cat was too old to get up to its former bird-hunting pranks,
and Arnold reflects that because Matthias saw Atossa only in her weak
old age, the canary formed the wrong idea of cats – for 'thou deemedst
cats were kind!' Yet, continues the poet, the cat was not merely kind – in
its full feline grandeur the cat was the equivalent of a complex human. It
was, indeed, comparable to the infamous Roman Emperor Tiberius.
Phrasing a couplet which sums up the feline nature with exquisite preci-
sion, Arnold insists that Atossa was:

> Cruel, but composed and bland,
> Dumb, inscrutable and grand,
> So Tiberius might have sat,
> Had Tiberius been a cat.

When faced with the need to describe or evoke the relationship between creatures, even such a poet as Arnold is reduced to viewing the cat in entirely human terms. 'Nearer human' was the cat's powers, 'closer knit' its life with ours. In investing the cat with human qualities, Arnold is not merely adopting a useful poetic convention: he is dealing with a most fascinating element in the feline nature – with that strange truth that there is something in the nature of the cat which reflects a higher level in the human psyche.

The cat is fundamentally a mystery – as much a mystery of space and time to modern man as it was to the Egyptians who made of her a goddess. The feline seems to promise the almost-tangible presence of a spiritual world, and is itself quite evidently susceptible to invisible spiritual influences. From this truth emerges the fact that the relationship between Cat and Man is a special one, for it hints at a curious symbiosis between the feline and human planes of existence, and points to the existence of a common spiritual link on some invisible plane of being. This ineffable sense of 'something higher' in the harmonious relationship between human and cat enters so frequently into the day-to-day communication between the two that it is often taken for granted by cat-owners. However we seek to describe this communication, we find that the normal distinctions which may be observed in relationships between man and the other animals seem somehow to be invalid. For example, the relationship is such that we may ask a question relating to the ordinary domestic cat which cannot be asked of any other animal or pet: does the cat own the owner, or does the owner own the cat?

Probably the answer to this wry question is six of one and half a dozen of the other, yet any cat-lover knows that the question is a valid one. Indeed it points to one reason why some modern psychologists trace a fairly clear spiritual link between owner and pet in terms of what is sometimes called an 'inner' connexion. From a recognition of this fact in modern times a special notion has emerged, in both psychological literature and popular cat-literature, of what is often called the 'psychic cat'.

The phrase is appealing, yet we should use it sparingly and with caution, for there is a sense in which there is no such creature as the specifically 'psychic cat'. All cats are psychic. All cats live in a spiritual realm normally inaccessible to human beings: when we use the phrase we are using circular language of the same kind as 'a feline cat' or 'a canine dog'. All cats have by predisposition access to levels of being, or to a level of spirituality, normally hidden to human beings.

The word 'psychic' is so much in use in certain quarters nowadays that we may easily forget that it is a very modern word. It was created, to denote supposed spiritual conditions, by people who had no knowledge of occultism, and who did not realize that within the occult terminology there were already more precise words which denoted the invisible realms far more accurately. Whatever words the psychologists might use, the occultist is unlikely to call the connexion between cat and owner 'psychic', for in occult terminology other words describe more precisely the invisible realm in which animals and humans meet. Even so, for the sake of glancing at this important domain we may as well use the popular word and refer to this relatively recently invented fiction, 'the psychic cat'.

Most of the words which the occultists would use to typify the spiritual nature of the cat need not concern us here, but one, derived from the Sanskrit, is now widely used in occult circles in place of terms of a far greater antiquity. This word is 'etheric'.

The etheric plane is that invisible plane where the life-force works into the material realm. I define it as 'invisible', but the truth is that under certain conditions, when for example a person is in a meditative state, it is quite possible to see something of this etheric. It is, however, extremely difficult to describe this plane with ordinary words simply because it does not have material characteristics, and while the experience of the etheric is strangely infused with a sense of familiarity, it is at the same time remote from our usual experience. Even so, those who have seen it (though 'experienced it' is a better phrase) describe it in terms of beautiful undulating rhythms, the flickering of quite unearthly lights, exquisite shifts of colour, and so on.

The etheric is sometimes called 'the plane of formative forces', for it is from this realm that the life-enhancing, and life-supporting, powers play into the material realm and invest it with life. This is reflected in one of the ancient alchemical terms for the etheric, the 'quintessence' or 'fifth element', which was higher than the four elements of Fire, Earth, Air and Water which gave rise to the phenomena of nature. The etheric was higher than nature, yet the source of its irrepressible life.

The realm is seemingly not subject to the ordinary limitations of matter, and has a different 'time' or 'duration', so that within the realm one not only has a different feeling of time, but there is also a distinctively different awareness of past and future. It is in some respects that realm in which time past and time future are gathered in an expansive present. In his attempt to deal with one aspect of the etheric, George Adams writes in his *Physical and Ethereal Spaces* of ethereal space as the realm of negative-Euclidean geometry, which is determined by a cosmic point that bears within it the germ and promise of a cosmic future. Such words, apt as they are, indicate how the ordinary vocabulary of communication begins to break down when one attempts to write about the etheric.

What has this elusive, fascinating realm of formative forces to do with the psychic, and with cats? Well, the occultist sees the cat as one of the creatures which is intimately linked with the etheric, as though this magical plane is more the dwelling of the cat than the physical. Much of the ancient Egyptian feline symbolism can be understood in a new way when this concept is grasped: the Egyptian goddess who links with the star-spangled night, whose eyes are the Sun and Moon, is a creature of the etheric. On a directly observable base, we may sense in the faultless movements of the cat, in its life of rhythmic grace, a revelation of the presence of an undiluted etheric force. On a more inaccessible level, the fact that cats have an ability to sense hidden danger, to apprehend something of the future and to see on planes normally hidden to human beings, to connote for the human a different sense of time, is another aspect of the feline connexion with the etheric. It is almost certainly this connexion between the feline and the higher realm of the etheric which explains why so many modern writers, bereft of the ancient terminologies to explain the magic of the cat, use the word 'psychic' to hint that the cat belongs to a world higher than that of familiar experience.

In terms of occult lore, all pets are supposed in some way or another to reflect the inner natures of their owners, to reflect a psychic link which is otherwise invisible. The cat is no exception, and is, indeed, a peculiarly intense example of this power to 'reflect' or mirror the owner. The notion of the cat as a psychic extension of its owner has become a part of the popular symbolism of cat-literature, in which cat and owner merge, change roles or wear one another's garb. It is the innate intelligence of Puss in Boots which leads his master to higher things, yet the fact that the Puss wears human clothing points to the deep symbolism of the tale. In the White Cat legends, which belong to the realm of folk psychology rather than to the occult, a girl is compelled to live for some years in the shape of a cat. It is, indeed, a 'type' of animal literature which has cats dress up as humans, and humans wear cat-skins, or change into cats. On the ordinary level, the symbolism is not particularly deep, for it merely attempts to express in distinctly materialistic terms the occult notion that there is a hidden realm of spirituality where feline and human merge, where cat and master are, if not equals, then at least beneficial to one another in a spiritual sense.

Human beings all too easily see cats as extensions of themselves, and are prepared to invest the creatures with human characteristics and spiritual qualities. No doubt the cat has the same inclination to see human beings in feline terms. In much the same way that a human is tempted to practise an unconscious anthropomorphism when looking at his cat, so, no doubt, the cat is tempted to practise an unconscious felinomorphism when looking at his owner. 'Chin up,' we might say to the despondent cat. 'Tail up,' the cat might reply, with just as much love. Even in this sense the seer becomes the seen, and the invisible worlds in which the cat and man live begin to merge. No wonder that some of the Egyptian sacred eye amulets are decorated with cats (figure 22), for when we look at the cat with our human eyes we see our own souls, and when the cat looks at us, it sees the feline world. Is the Udjat god-eye a feline eye looking at us, or does it represent a human eye looking at cats, with both human and cat bathed in the abiding light of Horus, to which the eye itself is said to belong?

In Paul Gallico's feline translation *The Silent Miaow*, written by an intelligent (if not to say smart-alec) domestic cat, we find an open confession that the cunning cat-author recognizes this human propensity to see the human in the feline race.

> I have mentioned the word 'anthropomorphism' [writes the cat] and defined its meaning in relation to us. It is most important where attitudes are concerned, since most people see and think of us not at all as cats, but rather as a kind of four-legged, fur-bearing human and in some mysterious way an extension of themselves.

Fig. 22   Designs with hieroglyphic cats on Egyptian amulets and seals

Well, this literate cat is quite right, since humans are usually prepared to see cats in anthropomorphic terms. However, we may suspect that this cat author is being feline-smug, or perhaps merely Machiavellian, when she instructs her cat-readers to encourage this human attitude. Her argument is that this instinctive anthropomorphism prevents owners from realizing the extent to which the cat has taken over the running of human households. The feline author is subtle enough to see that the vision we have of the world is determined by our unconscious attitudes and preconceptions.

Is the cat an extension in space and time of some inner human quality or psychological disposition? The occult literature would insist that this is the case, though not in such obviously materialistic terms as we might at first imagine. The cat, insists the occultist who has studied the secrets of biogeny, is the embodiment of a human quality which had to be given an external form. In terms of occult theory, each of the animals is an embodiment of some inner quality or vice which had to be, as it were, shed by human beings during the struggle to develop specifically human qualities.

This occult theory, which hints at the depth of relationship between man and the animals, and which admits a far closer spiritual tie between the two groups than is generally realized, is perhaps too complex to discuss in a few sentences, but the essence of the view is contained in the notion that all animals represent the embodiment of forces which were once, in the very distant past, part of the human being. Animals are the liberated fragments of human propensities. The problem with this occult view is that it is not easily grasped by modern readers: this is because it is almost diametrically opposed to the Darwinian view which has such a hold over contemporary thinking. While Darwinians might say that man evolved from a group of beings something like apes, the occultists would say that man and apes had a common spiritual ancestry. Darwinism represents a materialistic view of evolution, and its adherents are prepared to scrabble in the earth in search of evidence of man's origin. The occult view of evolution postulates a spiritual origin to all things, and the occultists therefore look to the cosmos for the origin of man and animals, realizing that they will find no material remains of their physical bodies in the earth, since early man, and the more sensitive early animals, did not have physical forms.

Occultists tell how there was a time, long before what the specialists call the Lemurian epoch (which preceded the more well-known age of

Atlantis), when man lived as a spiritual being without a physical body. During this period he had within his being many propensities and desire-entities which would render him savage were he not to rid himself of them. Longing to improve himself, he attempted to persuade these unwanted things to quit his being, and when he gradually did slough them off, they gradually found their own embodiment. As the world became more dense, and as man developed a physical body, the 'psychic rejects' of the humans began to develop their own physical forms, and became the forerunners of what we now call the animals. The animals were the first to descend into material form, to clothe themselves in physical matter. This no doubt explains why in the Book of Genesis, we find the animals being created before the male-female which preceded the creation of Adam and Eve (Chapter 1, 24–27). This view of the descent of man, as a descent from the spiritual realms rather than an evolution upwards from animal forms, explains why animal remains are found in the earth relating to geological epochs presumed to date from periods long before man came to earth. 'Came to earth' is the relevant phrase, however, for while the animals dwelled in a more or less material body, man existed on the earth in a spiritual form, which has left no imprint in the early records of the strata. One might as well seek the records of gusts of wind in the lower strata of the earth, as seek for the human form in the remote past.

This occultist view, which is far more complicated than the above simple statements would suggest, has a consequence. If it is true that man and animal were once spiritually related, then it is also true that man has a responsibility for the animals, since, on a spiritual plane at least, they are part of himself. Man is free to love or reject this shadow-life of his former self – he may tame animals, teaching them to be his servants or pets, or he may force them into further depths of bestiality, by allowing them to go wild or by hunting them. The one who sets out to love animals in the right way will take certain species as pets, and learn about aspects of love in this way: those who do this will consciously or unconsciously realize that they are redeeming something which belongs to themselves. He or she may even stop eating meat, on the basis that you cannot at the same time love and eat animals. This is one reason why so many occult groups practise vegetarianism.

Just as a flower could not have a continued existence without a bee, the occultist would argue, so the human being could not have a continued existence without the animal kingdom, and without developing the ties between the two by an unconscious programme of taming, training and ownership. The invisible and inexorable chains which link man with the animal kingdom are as subtle, powerful and ecologically necessary as those which connect flower and bee, making of plant and insect an ecological unity which has different freedoms, different life-styles, yet which need each other to continue their individual existences.

We may see from this that the taming of animals is involved with a deep spiritual symbolism, and in occult literature this symbolism is nowhere more explicit than in the idea of taming tigers or wolves in order to turn them into cats and dogs. Most occultists would agree that the purpose of world evolution is for man to learn the secret of universal love. It is sometimes said that before you can learn to love God in the right way, you have to learn to love humans in the right way – yet before this is possible one must learn to love oneself in the right way. To this must be added the less obvious truth that before one may learn to love oneself in the right way, one must learn to love animals. Seen from an occult point of view, therefore, keeping animals as pets is one of the sacred pathways by which man learns to love God.

From an occult point of view, then, those who actively love their pets, and attempt to establish a harmonious relationship with animals, are already learning the secrets of universal love. Whether they know it or not, all cat lovers are already on the road towards that understanding of universal love which is the fundamental aim of the serious occultist. However, even within the exciting framework of spiritual growth, the cat is an exception.

The reason why the cat has such an attraction for the human being is because the cat represents a densification of a part of the human soul which was beautiful as well as cruel, that part of the human being which is:

> Cruel, but composed and bland,
> Dumb, inscrutable and grand.

It requires little imagination for one to sense how beautiful we human beings would be if we had the grace of a cat. The finest ballerina must sacrifice most of her life, discipline her passions and body, to attain a semblance of that grace which is the birthright of any cat. In this truth lies a great secret about the ancient history which binds together the human soul and the cat. When we look at other animals, we look at discarded elements of a previous self – we look towards our past. When we look at a cat, we have a glimpse of the inner potential of the human soul for grace, as though we look towards the future. In this lies the real secret of the archetypal cat of the Egyptian mysteries (Plate 4), which had the power to kill the lower snake.

This unconscious move towards universal love, and the development of the psychic ties which exist between man and animal, have given rise to many symbolic tales which reflect man's dependence upon the animal kingdom. Equally, the same things have been moulded into a number of consciously developed attitudes towards animals by those who have undertaken to explore their own inner worlds. The animals – and particularly the untamed tiger – have been adopted as symbols of the dark, untamed desires of man.

When the famous Indian yogi, Tiger Swami, was questioned by his visitors about his power over the jungle cats, he explained that it was a matter of attitude. 'You,' he said, pointing to his visitors, 'look upon tigers as tigers; I know them as pussy-cats.' One of those present laughs at his words, and admits that even while he himself might be able to impress his subconscious with the thought that tigers are pussy-cats, it might be more difficult to induce tigers to believe it. We in the West might be more inclined to side with the diffident visitor, and pale in the face of a savage tiger, yet is there not a truth in the notion that our own attitude to the world conditions the nature of that world? The cat, one of the most sensitive of creatures, may indeed be a barometer not of the outer world but of our own inner world. As Tiger Swami said to his visitors, before he told them his personal story, the body (and hence the material realm) is literally manufactured and sustained by mind.

The inner journey of Tiger Swami had been a highly symbolic one, yet it was an adventure story in its own right. In his youth he fought, conquered and tamed many fierce jungle tigers, yet he recognized all along that there are many kinds of tiger, some of which, as he said, 'roam in jungles of human desires'. This symbolism found its way dramatically into his own life when he was ordered by a prince to fight a newly caught tiger named Raja Begum, which some of the locals believed was an evil spirit, cursed by the gods and reincarnated as a tiger. It would remain in the form of a striped animal during the daytime, but when darkness fell it would change into demonic form. His dramatic fight with the tiger, though successful in strictly gladiatorial terms, changed his life completely, and he began to pay attention to his inner tigers and sought out a teacher who would help him, as he put it 'to subdue the beasts of ignorance roaming in the jungles of his mind'.

Some occultists would agree with Tiger Swami and maintain that the
world we construct around us is partly a reflection of our inner attitudes.
We are centres into which the whole periphery of the cosmos has been
poured: within this soul-centre, which seeks always to expand back into
the periphery at the edge of our vision, roam many creatures, some of
them beings of light and others beings of darkness, but the most wonderful of which is the cat. 'The archetypal cat knows its way about our inner
world, and can direct us to treasures lying hidden in the recesses of our
minds,' writes Patricia Dale-Green. Clearly, this occult opinion is part
and parcel of the Tiger Swami's view of reality.

Some occultists insist that the oft-observed fact that the owners of dogs
resemble their pets in appearance, are almost caricatures of them, is an
example of the truth that the animals we adopt as pets reflect the nature
of our own inner psychic state. This 'resemblance' between man and
dog is more of a material nature than a spiritual thing. In contrast, few
owners resemble the physical appearance of the cats they take as pets,
yet it is not unusual to find a spiritual correlation between the psyches
of pet and owner. One has no need to point to historical examples to
sustain this view – everyone who has a cat will understand the extent to
which a quality of their own inner life is reflected in the nature of their
pet cat. Some are almost mirrors of their owner's spiritual life or state of
mind. A spiritually troubled owner rarely has a peaceful feline: show me
a contented cat, and I will show you a peaceful owner.

There are exceptions – and what stories may be gleaned from such
exceptions – yet generally we find such a close spiritual correspondence
between owner and cat that we must take it for granted that true ownership exists on a psychic plane not visible to ordinary levels of perception.
Is the cat (that delightful fragment of the outer world) merely an
embodied fragment of an inner psychic propensity of the owner, a sort of
externalized symbol of spiritual value or worth? It is hard to answer
such a question without involving oneself in occult theories which are
complex in the extreme, yet we can well understand why some astrologers cast horoscopes for cats, as though they were creatures subject to the
same stellar and cosmic relationships as human beings, with that inner
life of soul and spirit which it is generally thought humans possess.
Some astrologers go even further, however, and cast joint horoscopes
for cats and for the owners, in which they trace planetary and nodal
connexions between the two different charts in order to explain the rela-

tionship between them. This form of astrology properly belongs to the specialized art of synastry, in which charts cast for lovers are compared to reveal psychic and other correspondences. When it is practised with one of the partners in the form of a cat, it is perhaps the extreme form of what Gallico's writing-cat called 'anthropomorphism'.

There are very many records of how the 'psychic cat' does more than reflect the nature of its owner, however. Being aware of the spiritual realm, the cat is in touch with the angels and the devils, one of the few truly clairvoyant creatures. The clairvoyant psychic cat is a little more than the street-wise cat of popular literature and even more than the cat of wisdom mentioned in esoteric literature – it is the cat which, like the feline family of Aesop's tale mentioned on page 70, sits safely in the trunk of a tree, poised between heaven and earth. The clairvoyant cat is a psychopomp, with the power to lead man both into the infernal regions and out again. At times the psychic cat is perilously close to looking something like the demonic cat, which we shall deal with in chapters 6 and 7 – but this is only because, being psychic, it is alert to all the different levels of being which surround man on every side.

Since it undoubtedly lives in a spiritual realm which is not accessible to ordinary people, the cat is sometimes alert to dangers which are manifest on this 'psychic plane' long before they become evident on the coarser material plane. Because of this advantage of 'higher awareness', or insight, a devoted pet may sometimes alert its owner to dangers which would otherwise be unrecognized. Literally hundreds of examples have been put on record of how the pet cat, reacting to its psychic sensitivity, has helped its owner. In his interesting book *Incredible Cats*, David Greene gives several rather dramatic examples of such psychic aid and ability to save human life when disaster threatened, including some striking stories of how cats, seemingly sensitive to the dangers of coming air-raids during the Second World War in Britain, would warn their owners so that they might take cover (naturally along with their pets!) in the bomb-proof shelters. Among the true stories of cat-sensitivity recorded by Greene is that of the Italian cat, Toto. Aware of a threatening danger in the middle of the night when his owners were sleeping, Toto woke his master by repeatedly scratching his cheek, and then troubled him further until the man was persuaded that some sort of danger was afoot. As a consequence, the man woke his wife to discuss the matter with her, and eventually they decided to take their family to another part of the region, some distance from the sides of Mount Vesuvius where they were then lodging. They did not know then – but presumably Toto did – that exactly one hour later Vesuvius would erupt, burying in lava the village in which they had previously been sleeping.

Perhaps more important than these relatively rare dramatic stories of life-saving, however, are the numerous accounts of the ability we note in certain cats to exude a strange healing power. This ability has long been recognized by doctors and therapists, to a point where pets are sometimes recommended for old people in situations where calm and tranquillity will benefit health. The healing power of the cat was expressed in the Egyptian symbolism which emphasized the role of the cat as a serpent-killer, for the serpent was symbol of the death-force in the human realm, emblem of the dark forces of wisdom which give rise to illness. The notion was continued into Greek, Roman, Arabic and European cultures, often in a degenerate form, in the garbled spells and charms which regarded the parts of the cat, from the head to the tail, from the tongue to the claws, as having particular therapeutic qualities. We have already noted some of the magic and black-magic in which the dismembered parts of cats are said to cure, and these sordid recipes need no further elaboration. The modern psychologists are more directly holistic in their symbolism and methods, for they recommend the use of living cats, whole in fur, limb and spirit, to focus the attention of people who are autistic or in a state of near coma.

Among the most touching of the healing cases from the realm of psychology and medicine is that of the Mexican girl Maria, who was gradually led out of a seemingly endless coma by the appearance of a mysterious small cat in her bedroom in July 1976. The kitten, later christened 'Miguel', began to lick Maria's fingers, and returned night after night until Maria came out of her coma and began to speak to her parents. When she was sufficiently cured to be taken on holiday, Miguel disappeared as mysteriously as he had come.

A more homely example of the healing cat is noted by the Reverend Wood, when he writes about his blue-grey cat Prettina, whom he called Pret for short. During his long illness the cat established herself as head nurse:

> It was truly wonderful to note how soon she learned to know the different hours at which I should take medicine or nourishment; and during the night, if my attendant were asleep, she would call her, and, if she could not wake her without such extreme measures, she would gently nibble the nose of the sleeper, which means never failed to pro-

duce the desired effect. Having thus achieved her purpose, Miss Pret would watch attentively the preparation of whatever was needed, and then come and with a gentle purr-purr announce its advent to me.

The most marvellous part of this matter was, her never being five minutes wrong in her calculations of the true time, even amid the stillness and darkness of night. But who shall say by what means this little being was enabled to measure the fleeing moments, and by the aid of what power did she connect the lapse of time with the needful attentions of a nurse and her charge? Sure we have here something more than reason.

The never-failing accuracy of this wise little Cat was the more surprising, because she was equally infallible by night or day. There was no striking clock in the house, so she could not have been assisted by its aid; nor was it habit, for her assiduous attentions only began with the illness, and ceased with the recovery of the invalid. Instinct, popularly so called, will not account for this wonderful capability so suddenly coming into being, and so suddenly ceasing. Surely some spirit-guiding power must have animated this sympathetic little creature, and have directed her in her labour of love.

Although occultists would deny the reality of such a concept as the psychic cat, the unworldly or unreal or 'spiritual' cat seems to find its way into symbolism, art, literature and folklore in an extraordinary variety of forms, as previous accounts in this present book have already indicated. Since the phrase 'psychic cat' has no specific meaning, it has been twisted to mean very many different things. The 'ghostly cat', the 'healing cat', the 'sensitive cat' – even the 'occult cat' – has been called the 'psychic cat' by modern writers, ever since the word psychic was first used in this sense at the end of the nineteenth century. Yet if the phrase is to have any precise meaning, it can only be applied to the first of these – to that cat which appears to have an existence on a plane removed from the familiar world of normal experience.

This type of 'psychic cat' has been noted by some authorities as a possible source for the Cheshire Cat of Carroll's *Alice in Wonderland*. Apparently at Congleton, in Cheshire (not far from Daresbury), the ghost of a white cat has been seen. This psychic manifestation was observed by many people during the nineteenth century, and has even been recorded on separate occasions in our own century. The creature appears to have made a practice of sitting on a post near the remains of Congleton Abbey. However, as soon as it was approached by humans it would jump into the air and disappear. When the story (first recorded in literature at the beginning of this century) was investigated it was found that the cat had once been the pet of a Mrs Winge, a housekeeper in the old Abbey at Congleton.

The Winge cat must have had an accident, for when it returned to the home of its mistress one evening it was in spirit form, sitting placidly on the steps of her cottage but refusing to enter. When urged into its home by Mrs Winge the cat slowly vanished, even while she looked at it. Each evening the cat would return, sit on the step of the doorway, and then disappear, no matter how many friends and neighbours had gathered to watch the strange event. Although the Congleton ghost cat existed before Carroll wrote *Alice*, there is no real evidence (other than the proximity of Congleton to Daresbury) to show that he knew about the disappearing cat, and used it as the prototype for his own strange feline.

In his entertaining book on animal ghosts, Elliott O'Donnell admits that the most common forms of spirit phenomena seen in houses are ghostly cats. He claims that from personal experiments made in haunted houses he has been able to prove to his own satisfaction that the cat acts as a 'reliable psychic barometer'. It is a happy phrase, for many cat-owners will confirm that their pets are extremely sensitive to disturbances on the psychic plane, and there are very many true stories of how the cat responds to appearances of ghosts or psychic entities, or of how the dead cat will return 'in spirit' to its favourite place. A good example of this type of story is that told by the Italian psychic researcher Ernesto Bozzano about a case he had studied relating to the death of a cat which took place in the first decade of the present century.

The lady herself had a strong fear of cats (the technical term for this is ailurophobia), but an invasion of mice in her home required that she acquire a cat, which she did reluctantly, leaving it in the charge of her domestics. The cat appears to have performed its function well, but one day it started to have fits, and the servants of the house obtained permission to drown it. The lady herself continues with the story:

> The evening of the day that the animal had been destroyed, I was alone in the dining room immersed in reading, when suddenly I was impelled to raise my eyes, and look beside the door. I saw, or I seemed to see, that the door slowly opened, and permitted the entrance of the cat which had been sacrificed that morning. It was the same without doubt; but it seemed meagre, and was completely drenched, and streaming with water. Only the expression of its gaze was not the same, for it regarded me with human eyes, so sad that I was pained.

Plate 1 Cat in tree – an enduring
symbol of the clever-cunning cat,
practising her single art of survival.
From a sixteenth-century edition of
Aesop's Fables – 'The Cat and
the Fox'

Plate 2 (opposite) A cat, previously transformed by Venus into the shape of a woman, reveals her true nature. Illustration by Arthur Rackham from 'Venus and the Cat', in the 1912 edition of Aesop's Fables

Plate 3 (right) The 'Judas Cat' being fed bread (symbolic of the Sacrament) by Judas. Detail of a fifteenth-century tapestry depicting The Last Supper, *in the Uffizi, Florence*

Plate 4 (below) The Egyptian Cat, representative of the solar and stellar forces of light, slaying the Apep serpent of darkness, in the papyrus of Hunefer: from the Wallis Budge edition of the Egyptian 'Book of the Dead'

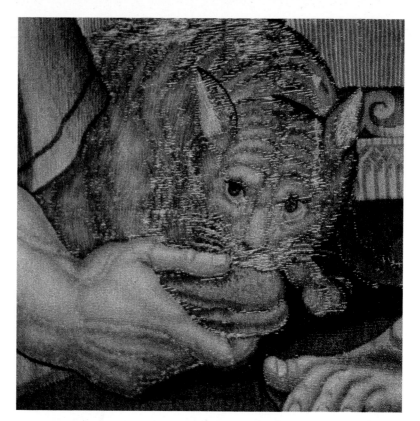

Plate 5 The mediaeval image of the cat as the witch's familiar, from a hand-coloured engraving by Maleuvre, after a drawing from a design by Queverdo, 'Depart Pour le Sabat'. The fact that the cat familiar (de rigueur *in images of witches*) is sitting on two beams of wood casually arranged in the form of a cross is intended to symbolize the contemporaneous notion that the rites of witchcraft were involved with the mockery of Christian ritual and beliefs

Plate 6 Statue to Perrault in the Tuileries Gardens, Paris, with his most enduring creation, Puss in Boots, striding jauntily at the base

Plate 7 The feline-headed demon Flauros, derived ultimately from the imagery of the cat-headed Egyptian Sekhmet. A hand-coloured woodprint from the 1864 edition of Collin de Plancy's Dictionnaire Infernal

Plate 8 The cat crest on the heraldic device of Coventry City, from the arms above the entrance to the Town Hall, Coventry

Plate 9 Cat-head on the memorial tablet to Thomas Ferrers (died 1970). Sculptured by John Protheroe and set in the north wall of the chancel of St Michael's Church, Baddesley Clinton

Plate 10 The cat watching the salmon – a representation of one of the repeated earth lives of the hero Bran. Illustration by Arthur Rackham to James Stephen's Irish Fairy Tales, 1920 edition

Plate 13 (opposite) The constel-lation of the Cat (Faelis), created by Lalande in 1805, between the constellations Antila Pneumatica and Hydra. From Lalande's Bibliographie Astronomique, *1805 edition*

Plate 15 (above) Feline head (probably that of a lioness) on the door of a house in Via Torta, Florence

Plate 14 (left) Chinese coin used in the consultation of the predic-tive method of the I Ching, or Book of Changes, *showing the twelve zodiacal animals*

Plate 16 The Moon card (back and front) from the tarot design by Kuykendall for the Tarot of the Cat People. *Copyright Karen Kuykendall, 1985*

Plate 17 Hieronymus Bosch, The Garden of Heavenly Delights. *Beneath the tree of paradise (behind Adam) a cat stalks off with what appears to be a dead rat in its mouth.* The Prado, Madrid

Plate 18 *A cat (through doorway) associated with the sin of Pride. Detail from the 'table top' panel of* The Seven Deadly Sins *by Hieronymus Bosch.*
The Prado, Madrid

Plate 19 *Cat being beaten by cupids, from an enamel by Couly Nouailher in the Bargello, Florence. The imagery is almost certainly designed to evoke the Christian theme of the maltreatment of the Lamb of God*

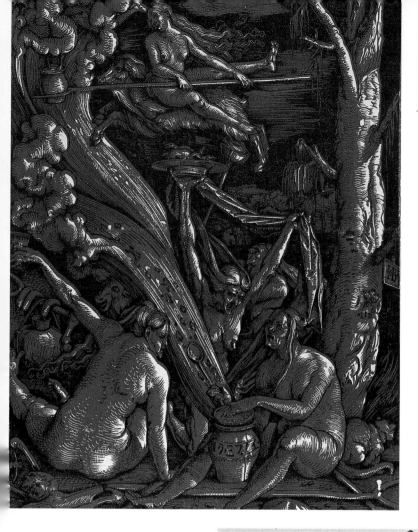

Plate 21 Hans Baldung Grien, Die Hexen *(1510), with transvecting witches, spell-making witches, and familiar cat*

Plate 20 The demon Bael, with the triple-heads of cat, human and toad. From the 1863 edition of Collin de Plancy's Dictionnaire Infernal

Plate 22 Detail of hand-coloured 'familiar' in the form of a demonic cat named Sathan, or Satan, who figured in the Chelmsford witch-craft trials of 1579. From the contemporaneous tract dealing with the trials and hangings of those found guilty

Plate 23 Illustration from Natha-nial Crouch's Kingdom of Dark-ness, 1688, showing the witch Anne Bodenham divining the future with the aid of dancing demons, a cat and a dog

Plate 24 Detail of the hand of the effigy of Lady Ann in St Michael's Church, Edmondthorpe. The left hand of the effigy is broken and the wrist stained dark red by some ferrous substance. Lady Ann was reputed to have been a witch, wounded in what occultists call 'repercussion': local legends tell how she was accustomed to turning herself into the form of a cat, and while she was so materialized her own butler, anxious to rid the kitchens of the creature, struck it with a meat cleaver, and wounded it in the paw. When the cat returned to its human form the wound was seen in the same place on Lady Ann's own hand. This 'wounded hand' was, by all popular accounts, transferred to her effigy

Plate 25 Cat-faced gargoyle with inscribed magical symbol of a spiral, on the south wall of the parish church at Littleborough, Lancashire. Although the spiral-symbolism is rare, the use of the cat imagery in gargoyles, soffits and surface decorations in ecclesiastical architecture is not uncommon

Plate 26 Lilith of the Seven Tales, *by Fay Pomerance, 1986. The artist, especially interested in Hebraic, Cabbalistic and Egyptian imagery, is representing an ancient theme in a new light, seeking to link the Hebrew demon Lilith, the first consort of Adam, with the feline 'goddess' tradition, in a meaningful symbolism.*

Private collection

Suspecting that the cat had not been drowned after all, she called her maid to remove it. However, the maid could not see the cat, which for the lady remained as 'plain and solid, as the table or the chairs'. The maid then said that she had been present when the kitchen-boy had carried it dead into the garden for burial. After the maid had gone, the cat slowly disappeared and was seen no more.

The sensitivity of the cat to strange, dangerous or occult situations, and its legendary 'second sight' is revealed in hundreds of similar stories, perhaps the most pithy of which is that recorded in a letter to the *Occult Review* of April 1924, which told how a friend of the writer had seen the spirit of one of her relatives sitting in a chair. Her own cat came into the room and immediately sprang into the lap of the spirit: it was shocked to find that the lap would not hold it, and 'fell to the floor greatly dismayed'.

The cat Mysouff, who was the familiar of the French writer Alexandre Dumas *père*, has gone down in cat history because of the number of times his strange psychic faculty has been noted in books on cats. Dumas himself tells us that each morning, when he set out to walk to his estate office, where he worked for the future king Louis Philippe, the cat would accompany him from his home in the rue de l'Ouest as far as the corner of rue de Vaurigard. Each afternoon the pet would meet him in the same place and conduct him home. There is perhaps nothing extraordinary in that performance, yet what is quite special, and a sign of the powerful psychic ability of Mysouff, was that whenever Dumas left his office at the appointed hour, Mysouff would scratch at the door to be let out in order to be on time to meet him – yet, strangely enough, whenever Dumas was unable to leave the office at the usual time, the cat would not stir.

The Reverend J. G. Wood revealed his special love for cats in his fascinating three-volume account of the natural history of the animal kingdom. Wood was far from being an occultist, yet he records several stories about his favourite creatures which reveal their sensitive and psychic nature. The long eulogy which Wood offers to his cat Pret, 'the most accomplished and singular Cat that ever caught a mouse or sat on a hearth-rug', is a classic of its kind, and essential reading for any cat-lover. She was by no means an exceptionally psychic cat, yet Wood noted her sensitivity to the static electricity which was present in human hair. This probably accounted for the fact that if a hair from her mistress's head were laid upon her own fur:

the Cat would writhe about on the floor and twist her body into violent contortions, and would endeavour with all her might to shake off the object of her fears. Even the mere pointing of a finger at her side was sufficient to make her fur bristle up and set her trembling, though the obnoxious finger were at six inches' distance from her body.

Wood came to the conclusion that this charge of electricity in the cat's body was one reason why people afflicted with rheumatism often found their sufferings alleviated by the presence of one of these 'electrically gifted animals'. A more dramatic 'psychic' story recorded by Wood concerned the burning of Peebles mill in 1853.

A family had lived for some time on the south side of Cuddie Bridge, and when they changed their home to the opposite side they had to leave behind their cat, which refused to budge from her usual haunts. Disliking the new inmates of her old home, however, pussy took possession of Peebles mill, where she lived for about eighteen months:

> On the 18th of October, 1853, at ten o'clock in the evening, as the former owner of the Cat was standing by the church porch, his attention was caught by the fugitive Cat, which was purring and rubbing herself against his legs as affectionately as in the olden times. He took the Cat in his arms, and when he attempted to put her down, she clung tightly to his breast, and gave him to understand in her own feline language that she was going home with him. Six hours after this return of the wanderer the mill was discovered to be on fire, and in a short time it was reduced to a heap of blackened and smouldering ruins.

Similar stories could be repeated by the thousand, and they all serve to point to the cat as a most extraordinarily psychic creature. One further history is worth recording, since besides being one of the most bizarre true 'cat-ghost' stories to emerge from the United States, it serves to point out the extent to which the dog is less sensitive to psychic phenomena than the cat.

The story was first reported in the *Weekly Dispatch* of 3 April 1921 in an article which gave a résumé of the strange case of the Ferryford ghost. So fearful were the locals in this small New Jersey village of their resident ghost, and so acute was the nervous tension, that the police had thought it advisable to order a precautionary confiscation of all firearms.

The Ferryford spectre was that of John Koch, who had kept the motor repair shop in the village, and who had killed his mechanic during a quarrel before committing suicide. For some time afterwards the spirit of Koch, accompanied by an enormous white cat, was seen to enter the living room of the cottage in which he had lived, and caused widespread consternation among those visiting his widow and her family. The *Weekly Dispatch* continues the tale:

> Last night fourteen people, headed by the local policeman, formed a ring round the cottage, determined to solve the mystery. Among them was a man from whom Koch borrowed money the day before his death, and a dog – the latter to investigate the spectral cat. Shortly after midnight, a loud crash was heard in the cottage. Entering, the watchers found a portrait of the dead man's mother-in-law on the floor. Then a hollow laugh was heard, and Koch appeared at the window surrounded by what was described as 'a faint blue mist'. On a small pear tree behind him was a large white cat with long whiskers. With a loud bark the dog made for the cat as it sprang to the ground. But to the dog's amazement he passed right through the cat, and his jaws snapped in empty air. Feeling unequal to the situation, the dog uttered a low howl and fled. Meanwhile . . . the remainder of the party bombarded the 'ghost' with lamps, flat-irons, and other things.
>   But the spectre merely smiled sardonically, called the cat, and faded away.

Of course, the dog-lover may contend that although the dog has its feet more firmly on the earth than the cat, it is equally sensitive to psychic phenomena, and one must admit that there are many spirit-dog stories to confirm this view. In fact, it has often struck me that there are far more psychic photographs of dogs than cats. I can give no explanation for this, save perhaps the suggestion that cat owners sense that their feline companions survive into a spiritual realm and feel no real need to drag them back to the material realm in the form of psychic pictures to comfort their grieving selves. Dog-owners, on the other hand, are notoriously more materialistic, less attuned to the psychic realm than the majority of cat-lovers, and seek some material confirmation that their dogs have an afterlife. After all, there is nothing more 'spiritually materialistic' (to use Chogyam Trungpa's splendid phrase) than photographs of the dead, for the dead are spiritual beings living in a higher world, while normal photographs record only light falling on emulsion. Such photographs merely confirm the unproven prejudice that after death there exists a spiritual body of more or less the same appearance as the physical body. Whether this spiritual body has anything to do with the departed spirit may be called into doubt – indeed in some cases the evidence would suggest that it could well be a simulacrum used by other discarnate entities for their own purposes. The first of the great spiritualists, Andrew Jackson Davis, warned his readers about this very thing, advising them to distinguish carefully the spirits which confront them in seance rooms and in their other investigations.

While occultists admit that one of the spiritual forms does to some extent resemble the physical earthly body for a while, it denies that this 'copy' continues on the astral plane for very long. According to this well-informed view, therefore, there is something innately suspicious about so-called 'spirit photographs' when the psychic phenomena have been removed from the material world for some length of time.

However, some of the finest animal 'spirit photographs' are of creatures not very long dead. I put the term 'spirit photographs' in inverted commas, for those specialists in this history of the subject insist that the proper term should be 'soul' or 'psychic' photographs, for according to occult theory the spirit itself does not take on a sufficiently materialistic form to be recorded on film, while the mediating soul may. Again, the animal itself does not have a spirit, though it does have what we may term a soul. I have already touched on the occult theory of Group Soul on pages 13–15, however, and need not repeat myself here.

One of the most extraordinary psychic photographs of a cat was taken in the August of 1925 by Major Wilmot Allistone while he and his family were staying at a pension in Clarens, Switzerland. The photograph itself is a somewhat badly composed family group, with the mother or nurse standing behind the pram, one child inside it, and another (seemingly interested in something other than his father and the camera) standing in front. When the roll-film was developed and the frame printed Major Allistone was astonished to observe that an enlarged portion of the boy in the foreground showed the image of a ghostly kitten (figure 23) nestling against the more substantial toy rabbit which the boy holds in his left hand. There had been no kitten in the boy's arms when the photograph was taken. So far as it is possible to judge, the boy is not actually holding the body of the cat, so that its head remains like some ghostly imitation of the fading Cheshire Cat of *Alice* without the attendant grin. The appearance of this head is altogether different in quality from the rest of the details in the photograph: for example, the head is virtually transparent, and the shadows which enable one to see the form are in no way as intense as the shadows of the hand or the toy rabbit.

Fig. 23   Detail of family photograph, showing the ghostly head of a cat. Picture taken by Major Wilmot Allistone in 1925

The interesting thing is that Major Allistone recognized the translucent head of the kitten as resembling that of a white kitten which had belonged to the family, and with which his boy was accustomed to play. The unfortunate kitten had been badly mauled by a St Bernard dog some weeks before the picture was taken, and had died a short while afterwards. The picture survived mainly by chance, for Major Allistone was interested in the occult teachings of Madame Blavatsky, and her Theosophy, as a result of which he decided to send the photograph to the Society for Psychical Research in London for investigation. No explanation for the appearance of the kitten was found. Fraud was certainly out of the question, and a stereoscopic microscope showed that the original negative was genuine. The picture and the Society's report were lost in a file of letters for some decades until I chanced to discover it while sorting out correspondence relating to psychic photography in 1976.

Another equally fascinating psychic photograph involving a cat was taken in a similar accidental way by Alfred Hollidge at Leigh-on-Sea, Essex, in June 1974. The flash-exposure picture was intended to show the Hollidge family cat Monet in her familiar position in front of the fire, and there was some delay in the processing of the colour film as there were still several frames to be used up. During that period Mr Hollidge was taken ill, and eventually died in the September of the same year.

When Mrs Hollidge eventually opened the packet of prints she was surprised to see running in front of Monet a curious 'extra', perhaps a ghostly kitten, with an odd line running from its body and across the hearth-rug (Plate 12). The Hollidge family had only one cat, and there was certainly no other cat in the house when the photograph was taken. The alert suspicion with which Monet views the intruder indicates that, even if Mr Hollidge did not see the extra when he took the picture, his cat certainly did.

The Monet picture reminds one of the true story recorded by Paule V. Hampso in *The Cat-Lover's Journal* of 1974–5, about her cat Dina which had been killed by a car. As replacements the family bought two Brown Burmese which were named Aquarius and Scorpio (two very psychic names, one notes). At about 10.00 one evening, when the family had relatives for dinner, the hackles of these two cats suddenly rose several inches, while they stared intently at the basket which had been previously used by Dina. They were spitting furiously, their backs raised, and continued in this way for four or five minutes. After their guests had gone, Mrs Hampso's husband remarked that during the fracas he had seen Dina sitting in her basket, gazing around the room with untroubled eyes and eventually fading away into nothingness.

One of the most famous psychic felines was never photographed, but its haunting was sufficiently well attested to for it to be given the title 'the Killakee Cat', or the 'Black Cat of Killakee', and it remains one of the few psychic cats to have merited a portrait. According to the modern writer Dennis Bardens, accounts of the sighting of this demonic cat in the Dower House at Killakee in Ireland, which has the reputation of being haunted by several quite conventional spectres as well as the demonic feline, are said to go back to the eighteenth century. Dennis Barden deals with the occult associations of the place in his *Psychic Animals*, so I shall mention here only the strange accounts of the Killakee Cat in its modern sighting.

Relatively ancient as records of this cat appear to be, the most graphic accounts of its appearance are those given by the artist Tom McAssey, whose personal experiences were preserved in *The Dublin Evening Herald* in December 1968. McAssey was painting in the gallery of the Dower House when the locked door mysteriously opened. He went to investigate, and he saw a shadowy figure in the hallway. Thinking that someone was playing a trick, he shouted an invitation for the person to enter:

'Come in; I see you.'

A low voice replied, 'You can't see me.'

After a moment or two, McAssey slammed the heavy door and retreated. Halfway down the gallery he looked back and saw a monstrous black cat, its red-flecked eyes fixed upon him.

Later that same day, McAssey returned to his room and painted the creature exactly as he had seen it: in the recorded account of the story it is said that the picture of the apparition was later put on permanent display in Killakee Art Centre. Perhaps the most striking thing about this graphic account of a demonic cat is the fact that, had it occurred in earlier times, this creative artist might have suffered a fate very different from having his picture exhibited in a local gallery: in earlier days even the sight of a psychic or demonic cat was enough to have the person himself hanged. The examination of Dorithy Ellis on 30 May 1647 recorded by the historian Cecil L'Estrange Ewen is a fairly typical account of how the demonic cat could lead to such execution.

> [Dorithy Ellis] saith that about thirtie years since shee being much troubled in her minde there appeared unto hir the Devell in the likness of a great catt and speak unto this examinee and demanded of hir hir blood which she gave hime after which the spirit in the likness of a catt sucked upon the body of this examinee and the first thing that this examinee commanded her spirit to doe was to goe and be witch 4 of the cattel of Tho. Hitch all which cattel presently died and further this examinee confesseth that she sent hir catt spirit to bewitch and take away the life of Marie the daughter of Tho. Salter of Stretham . . .

In the 'Depositions of York Castle' we find a record of 14 October 1654 which charges Elizabeth Roberts, the wife of a joiner at Beverley, with witchcraft. The one bringing the accusation claims:

> that on Saturday last, about seven in the evening, Elizabeth Roberts did appear to him in her usuall wearing clothes, with a ruff about her neck, and presently vanished, turning herself into the similitude

of a catt, which fixed close about his leg, and after much struggling, vanished, whereupon he was much pained at his heart. Upon Wedenesday there seized a catt upon his body, which did strike him on the head, upon which he fell into a swound or trance. After he received the blow he saw the said Elizabeth escape upon the wall.

Psychic cat, or Devil? Such records are so frequent and so typical of witchcraft literature that they are almost banal examples of depositions taken from men and women in the sixteenth and seventeenth centuries, when the cat was the form most favoured by the Devil, and when all domestic cats were suspect of being witch familiars. Nowadays, however, when ghostly (or even demonic) cats are seen on the spiritual plane they are no longer automatically regarded as minions of the Devil but merely ghosts caught out of their proper sphere, half in the spirit-world and half in this. The experience of ghostly or astral cats has probably not diminished; what has changed is the way this phenomenon is interpreted and understood.

The passage through the veil into the realm of death is often linked with the appearance of a cat – usually a black cat. In northern Italy it is still believed by some that when a man is ready to die, then Satan will pass in front of his bed in the form of any animal other than the lamb (this of course being the emblem of the Lamb of God, who is Christ). Most usually his demonic disguise is that of a goat, a cock or a cat – all creatures which the worst of the diabolical grimoires admit may be used in the sacrifices required to raise certain demons. In Germany it is said that if a cat is seen on a newly dug grave, then it is a sign that the departed spirit is in Hell. In some parts of France (especially in Normandy) it is believed that if a black cat crosses one's path in the moonlight, it is a presage of death.

From the realms of such superstitions, the *Proceedings of the Society of Psychical Research* (Vol. V, p. 156) bring us down to factual reality. Mrs E. L. Kearney tells how, in January 1892, as her grandfather lay ill, she was descending the staircase below his room when she saw in the passage a strange cat walking towards her. The cat hid itself behind a door in the corridor, and Mrs Kearney followed it into what was in effect a cul-de-sac, only to find that it had vanished. On the following day her grandfather died. Her mother then told her that on the eve of her own father's death, she too had seen a cat which walked around his bed, and also disappeared.

The link between the psychic cat and the Devil lingers unnoticed even in some modern phrases. For example, the 'cat's paw' is the rippling of the waters during a calm, indicative of a coming squall, as though some gigantic psychic cat is invisibly stirring the waters with her paw. Such a term may be derived from the old tradition that a frolicking cat indicates a coming gale, for in fishing communities the cat was often seen as an indicator of coming winds, storms and good or bad fishing times. In days when the distinction between a psychic cat and an ordinary cat was more blurred, the fisherman who saw a cat on his way to the morning's fishing would often return home, confident that the day would be wasted because of the bad omen.

Nor is the tradition limited to seamen of modern times. Many country-folk, for all their fondness for cats, still blur the distinction between the psychic and the real. The witchcraft murder trial of John Blymer, Wilbert Hess and John Curry at York, Pennsylvania, in January 1929 revealed the extraordinary fact that three-quarters of the population of York County were convinced of the validity of the same feline witchcraft magic as had been held to be true by their Moravian ancestors two centuries earlier. The *Sunday Express* for 13 January 1929 may be forgiven for the quite normal tones of journalistic high drama, yet behind the account one may read the facts of strange superstition which can be traced back to mediaeval recipes and witchcraft beliefs:

> The farm lands and cities of York County are in the grip of a witches terror, the villages fear-ridden at the thought of 'hexes' and evil spirits. The country barns, and the cowsheds and the cattle shelters bear strange crosses and painted hieroglyphics against the 'hex'. Black cats have practically disappeared from the countryside, for it is known that a sure way of making one's peace with Satan is to plunge one alive into boiling water, keeping the last bone for an amulet.

By means of such amulet-making the real cat is transformed into a psychic cat, with imagined magical powers which work on the psychic or astral plane. In his *Masque of Queens* the seventeenth-century playwright Ben Jonson makes it clear that less ephemeral matter than cats' bones were used in magical recipes, for his witches sing:

> I from the jaws of a gardener's bitch,
> Did snatch these bones and leaped the ditch;
> Yet I went back to the house again,
> Killed the black cat, and here's the brain.

The physical remains of the cat – be they bones or brains – have a special psychic quality to which vast numbers of magical treatises and grimoires attest; there is further consideration of these in chapter 6.

However, examples such as the relatively modern York County witch-craft trials, when shorn of their journalistic excesses, merely serve to indicate by their very divergence from the general view, how different the psychic cat of modern times is from that of the Middle Ages. In the modern world, for all the exceptions we note in York County, the psychic cat has been cleansed of its immediate diabolical associations. Even the black cat, the most feared of all the late-mediaeval witch familiars and demons, has become a good-luck charm; and indeed the notion that the sight of a black cat will inevitably lead to good fortune appears to go back to ancient Egyptian times.

Yet we cannot be sure whether the Devil has been expunged from our records and vision, or is merely lying doggo in the wings, aware that a hidden devil has more power of temptation than one in full view. When the modern scientific view of things chose initially to ignore the Devil in their survey of the world (presumably in the erroneous conviction that he was invisible or could not be weighed), they gradually convinced society that he did not exist. What could be more absurd than a PhD thesis on the scientific measurement of the Devil? Yet in earlier days the greater number of savants and natural scientists were concerned with the study of this Gentleman, and made much effort to understand the workings of his minions the lesser demons. With the rejection of the Devil as a suitable subject for investigation went the imagination of the black cat as a demonic being. But the place of such rejects is almost certainly what we now call the subconscious, and it is in this dark realm that the demons have their existence in modern times. Periodically our waking life is disturbed by the emergence, as from another space and time, of the psychic cat. Is the psychic cat merely the de-bugged demonic cat of former times?

Certainly the majority of modern accounts of psychic cats have not the slightest whiff of demonism about them. Dennis Bardens' interesting book on psychic animals contains several fascinating accounts of ghostly cats, but perhaps the most endearing is the one he collected from a series published by the *Daily News* in the 1920s relating to a small black cat which had to be painlessly destroyed because she had contracted a disease. Her wraith spirit returned to the house of her owners, however, and used to play by the bannisters on the landing, near the bedroom where she used to have breakfast with them every morning.

> A visitor to the house saw her frolicking with a doormat in a way she
> loved to do; and a maid met her on the stairs. I never have known a
> more intelligent little cat, nor one that loved her home and owners
> more, so it was of great interest to find that after death she came back
> in that way.

Very many accounts of ghostly cats have been preserved in journalistic 'first-hand' accounts published by *Psychic News* and even in the more
austere *Proceedings of the Society for Psychical Research*, of which the following are typical. In 1884 Mrs Griefenberg and her daughter were having
their lunch when they saw a large white Angora cat with green eyes
under the table. The cat prowled around the table, left by way of the door,
passed half way down the passageway and then turned to stare at the
women. As it did so, it dissolved into thin air. The same curious event
was repeated in Leipzig, and the two women prepared a document con-
firming their experience to be lodged with the Society in 1890.

In July 1909 an experience was recorded by a lady whose identity was
known to the Society, but who elected to remain anonymous. Her sister
had a favourite pure-bred Persian called Smoky. In the spring of 1909
she fell ill, and to compound matters she was worried by a dog: her ribs
were broken and she died in the middle of June. The body was buried by
the gardener.

> On July 6th, 1909, my sister and I were at breakfast, and I was reading
> a letter aloud to her. I was sitting with my back to the window, which
> was on my sister's left. Suddenly I saw her looking absolutely scared,
> and gazing out of the window. I said 'What is the matter?' and she
> said 'There's Smoky, walking across the grass!' We both rushed to the
> window and saw Smoky, looking very ill, her coat rough and staring,
> and walking lamely across the grass in front of the window, three to
> four yards from it. My sister called her, and she took no notice. She ran
> out after her, calling her.
>   I remained at the window and saw the cat turn down a path lead-
> ing to the end of the garden. My sister ran after her, still calling, but to
> her surprise Smoky did not turn or take any notice, and she lost sight
> of her among the shrubs.

The ghostly cat was seen by several other people on that day, and one of
the servants actually ran to get milk to feed the sick animal. The gardener was so indignant when he felt he was being accused of not bury-

ing the cat properly that he went back to the grave, took up the dahlias he had planted over it, and dug out the body of Smoky for all to see.

Oldfield Howey, well versed in occult lore, suggested that this psychic cat was not the actual ghost or soul of Smoky, 'but an astral photograph, which the sufferings of the cat had impressed on the psychic atmosphere'. Such stories of spirit appearances (whether as ghosts or 'astral photographs') are commonplace and are leapt upon by many psychics as 'evidence of survival', but whether they are evidence of survival or not remains unknown. They appear rather to point to the existence of another world – perhaps a soul-world – contiguous with our own world. But what survives in this realm from the earthly plane is, perhaps, anybody's guess. All we may be reasonably sure of is that the majority of psychic cats are of much the same friendly and feline disposition as their incarnate equivalents.

If the ghost-cat is indeed the true 'psychic cat', it is also a ghost which is found in the recesses of our own mind. We saw how this symbolism of the inner cat (which is, of course, the archetypal cat) was reflected in the life of Tiger Swami, who spent his life struggling with his inner and outer cats. The adventure-ridden symbolism of the yogi's inner fight is not unique, however. In the fascinating *Autobiography of a Yogi* by Paramhansa Yogananda, in which part of the story of Tiger Swami is told, we find reproduced a rare photograph of the monk Krishnananda with his tame vegetarian lioness, which lived on a diet of rice and milk, and which had been taught to utter the meditative word Aum, that sacred sound which reflects the three in one and the descent of the Word of God. Is the psychic symbolism of the cat somehow connected with the notion that the feline mewing is itself a clumsy attempt to say that word backwards – Mau – as a symbol of the seer seen?

The etheric cat is a mirror-reflection of the human soul, with all its yearnings, and with all its untamed elements of darkness swathed in grace. The true man is attempting to perfect the sound Aum, and the true cat is attempting to perfect the sound Mau. The cat is the celestial mirror-language of the human soul, and the taming of the tiger is an inner and outer activity by which the seer becomes the seen, and the hearer becomes the heard. Such a concept, allied to the fact that the truly tamed tiger becomes, in the words of Tiger Swami, 'a pussy cat', helps us to understand something of the deeper mysteries of our own nature, and of that mystery of mysteries, the ordinary domestic cat.

Chapter Five

THE SYMBOLIC CAT IN ART

his tears and praying,
By wizard charms and much soothsaying,
Wrought things so well, that Destiny,
One fine day, changed the Cat into a Woman.
...
Mad friends became mad lovers then;
And not the fairest dame e'er known
Had ever such affection shown
To him she'd chosen from all men.

AESOP
from the Fable of Venus and the Cat

The fable of Aesop which has the prayers of man turn a favourite cat into a lovely woman is in some respects an allegory of the artistic enterprise. The artist seeks to turn into a spiritual form acceptable to humanity those parts of nature which appear to be unredeemed. The artist is therefore both a god and a redeemer of the physical realm, who must pray to Venus that she will grant him the power to turn brute creature into creation.

When the artist chooses the cat as his model, then he is automatically walking with the archetypes, for the artistic creativity springs directly from the Sun, from the warm realm of zodiacal Leo, while the cat herself is from the Moon. Each time the artist takes up pen or brush to create a cat, he is entering into the most archetypal of relationships in which the Sun faces across the zodiac to light up the face of the dark moon. Perhaps this alone explains the wisdom of Aesop in choosing Venus as the goddess who grants human life to the cat, for Venus is the only feminine planet which is in orbit between the Sun and the Moon.

This fact of 'walking with the archetypes' when faced with the cat as subject may well explain the popularity of the cat with painters and poets – not merely the actual presence of feline companionship, but also the choice of the cat as subject matter. The fact that the cat is in many ways that aspect of the brute creation which is already nearest to man may explain why it is such a special symbol in art. It is indeed difficult to draw or paint a cat without expressing the mysterious life which flows from its innermost being. One is not clear whether the sphinx looks like the cat, or whether the cat looks like the sphinx, yet mystery pervades both, just as it pervades the earliest representations of the feline which have come down to us from Egyptian times. Even the simple Egyptian amulets, designed to evoke Bastet, are filled with grace in the few lines which depict the hieroglyphic form of the cat (figure 22). Thousands of such cat amulets have recently been uncovered in the Egyptian sands, and many of them – especially the Udjat amulets – have been catalogued by such archaeologists as Petrie. We shall examine the numerological significance of some of these amulets later (see Conclusion) and so for the moment can move from the tiny cat amulets to the colossal statue of Bastet with a cat's head, the whole figure six feet high, exclusive of the head disc and base, but with dignity innate in every contour of form. This Egyptian equivalent of Venus may not have turned feline into human, but for sure she has turned gross matter into a goddess. The historian may derive some satisfaction from the fact that this huge feline goddess was carved on the orders of Shishank, the first Egyptian king to be mentioned by name in the Bible, but the non-specialist will delight that the head represents all the characteristics of the cat, from the mysterious and aloof to the intense and spirited.

Time and again as we examine the cat as it has been figured into some deep or significant symbol, we shall note the ease with which the artist expresses grace, mystery, intensity, *joie-de-vivre* and sheer exuberance when he attempts through his art form to see into the nature of the cat.

The occult texts constantly re-emphasize how the importance of the cat lies in its association with the Moon, which is, from an occult point of view at least, in opposition to the Sun. Inevitably, most textbooks on astrology point to the cat as being under the dominion of the Moon. However, even before the full tradition of astrological lore had been introduced to Europe in the twelfth century, there is evidence that the connexion between the cat and the lunar cycles was recognized. One wonders to what extent the early Christian monks who used the cat in their imagery were aware that they were continuing a pagan tradition in linking the lunar cycle with the cat? Perhaps they had read their Plutarch, who had taken the interpretation of 'lunar cat' to the extreme by recording the tradition that the size of the cat's body increased and decreased with the waxing and waning of the Moon? Earlier writers had insisted that this increase and decrease with the lunar cycle applied only to the cat's eyes.

According to the secret tradition in the diagrams which portray the earth at the centre of the cosmic cycles, the earth itself is bathed in the circuit of the Moon – in what was in mediaeval times called the 'sphere' of the Moon, which was something altogether different from the Moon's physical orb or body. In the secret tradition it was recognized that at birth and death the soul or spirit of man had to pass through this lunar sphere in order to reach (or leave) the earth. This is one reason why the zodiacal sign Cancer, which is ruled by the Moon, is sometimes called the 'Gate of Birth'; for according to this concept the descending spirit of a newly born baby has just passed through the sphere of the Moon. In the same way, at death the spirit which relinquishes the physical body must pass through the same lunar sphere in order to find itself free in the planetary spheres beyond, eventually to reach the spiritual space of Heaven.

This belief in the importance of the sphere of the Moon is one reason why it was often claimed in occult circles that this sphere was the realm of Purgatory. Here the purgatorial demons dwelled, waiting to devour the impurities of the soul-life of anyone who passed through. Obviously, the soul of a child who was yet to be born was quite pure, so its passage through the sphere of the Moon involved no encounters with demons. However, few men die with their souls unsullied, and it is the darkening of the post-mortem soul which attracts the demons. This tradition explains why so many of the purgatorial symbols are lunar. In modern times the notion has been materialized somewhat (in accordance with modern materialistic ways of thinking) so that we find even esotericists linking the physical body of the Moon with the demonic or purgatorial realm: an example of this may be seen in the writings of P. D. Ouspensky.

The Celtic circular cross at Kirk Braddan on the Isle of Marn, which makes such obvious use of feline and lunar imagery, is designed to show that the Cross of Christ has dominion even over Hell. Indeed, during those momentous days before the Resurrection, Christ descended into the realm of Purgatory and Hell, to show that even these places (or 'soul-states') were subject to his power. Some of the esoteric documents which are now preserved in the so-called 'Apocryphal' texts of early Christian literature make it clear that the first beings to recognize fully the power of Christ were the demons, who were terrified when they realized that their dominion would eventually be at an end. In view of this, it is not far-fetched to see the Kirk Braddan cross in terms of this belief, for it proclaims that the Cross of Christ has dominance over even the sphere of the Moon. In this sense, it is well in accord with Christian beliefs, and not to be regarded as a survival from a pagan lunar cult. After all, we find a similar use of feline symbolism in the dominance of the high Cross over the two cats in the Monasterboice cross (figure 14). One cat is washing her kitten, presumably in reference to the belief that a kitten was born in the stable at the same time as Jesus, while the other is playing with a captive bird, presumably a symbol of the holy spirit. Between them, these two cats represent the extremes of feline symbolism in Christian imagery – the virginal 'White' cat, and the demonic 'Black' cat.

It was the French astronomer Joseph Jérôme Lalande who attempted to place the cat in the heavens (Plate 13). Some authorities say that he did this to spite Voltaire, distinctly not a cat-lover, who had argued that the cat did not know how to achieve a place among the constellations where such other animals as bears, dogs, lions, bulls and the like were secure. It was true that while there were thirty-three animals in the old sky maps, the cat had no place among them, so Lalande created a small constellation which he called 'Faelis', between Antlia Pneumatica (Air Pump) and Hydra (Plate 13). 'I am very fond of cats,' he wrote. 'I will let this figure scratch on the chart. The starry sky has worried me quite enough in my life, so that now I can have my joke with it.' The cat did not claw the chart for very long, for while it was adopted for the influential map published by Bode in the 1805 edition, it disappeared from later constellation maps, being, as the astronomer Camille Flammarion wrote, 'superfluous'.

There is even an Oriental explanation as to why the cat was not included in the Chinese zodiac. According to the old story, when Buddha was about to die, all the animals came to visit him to say farewell and to weep for his passing. The snake and the cat were the only two creatures not to weep: the cat's attention was drawn to a rat, which was weeping with the other animals, and she immediately pounced upon it and killed the unfortunate creature. This sacrilege, of taking a life during a sacred moment, is the reason given as to why the cat was not included in the zodiac. It is all the more surprising, therefore, to find the modern *Larousse Encyclopedia of Astrology* (1980) turning the fourth sign of the Chinese zodiac into a cat. According to the entry, the native is 'talkative, theatrical and rich in imagination, if somewhat vain and superficial'. In fact, the fourth sign of the Chinese zodiac is a Hare, corresponding to our own Cancer.

The coin in Plate 14 is a Chinese counter used for the magical process involved in consulting the divinatory text of the *I Ching*. On the obverse of the coin are the eight trigrams from which the sacred hexagrams of the Book of Changes are constructed. On the side visible in Plate 14 we see the symbols for the twelve zodiacal animals, and the Chinese characters for their corresponding branches. At the bottom of the coin is the Hare, which corresponds to zodiacal Cancer. From this Hare, running clockwise, we see the Dragon, Snake, Horse, Sheep, Monkey, Cock, Dog, Boar, Rat, Ox and Tiger. The only link with the cat in the Chinese system of occult beliefs, is the rulership of the Moon over the Hare sign, and the old Chinese notion that the 'face' we Europeans see in the Moon is actually a hare, a notion which appears in certain magical treatises of ancient China. The hare in the Moon is an alchemist's assistant, supposed to help in the preparation of the secret elixir of immortality. In this guise it is worshipped on the 15th day of the eighth lunar month.

We shall eventually note that during the mediaeval period the cat gained for itself such an evil aura that artists of that period were reluctant to adopt the creature as a symbol for anything other than evil. This appears to have entered into the realm of mythology in these periods, for we find that even in large-scale cycles involving literally hundreds of different animals and fabulous beasts, the cat is rarely included. We may note this, for example, in the surviving soffits in the long corridor which runs alongside the main exhibition rooms on the Arno side of the Uffizi. These were painted in the sixteenth century, and incorporate literally hundreds of different animals, birds, insects, fabulous beasts and grotesques, many of them linked by themes derived from alchemy, astrology and esoteric mythology; yet there does not appear to be a single representation of a domestic cat upon this ceiling. In one tiny detail, on the soffit which has at its centre the story of Jupiter's appearance in the form of a shower of gold, there is an animal which might well be a demonic cat, but this only goes to show how well entrenched was the reluctance in the late mediaeval tradition to use the tamed pussy cat as a symbol of anything but evil.

The lion symbol, on the other hand, was almost overused in alchemy. The most famous and widely used alchemical lion-images were the Green Lion and the Red Lion, symbolic forms employed in one of the most well-known of all alchemical texts, the *Rosarium Philosophorum* of 1550. These coloured lions denoted important stages in the process of making from crude matter the magical philosopher's stone, which was the whole business of this remarkable art.

The inner significance of these lions need not concern us here, for to fully understand their meaning it would be necessary to give a complete analysis of the *Rosarium*. It is perhaps sufficient to note that the text has resulted in a variety of compelling leonine images, which portray a lion swallowing or disgorging the Sun. In fact, the lion appears in many pre-sixteenth century alchemical texts in other symbolic disguises, mainly because alchemical symbolism is intimately linked with astrology. The white and red lions in the arcane illustration to Lambsprinck's book on alchemy in figure 24 represent spirit and soul, which were sometimes otherwise symbolized as Sun and Moon in both alchemy and astrology. This link between the lion and the Sun stems from the ancient occult tradition which has always viewed the lion as representative of the zodiacal sign Leo, which was itself ruled by the Sun. From the point of view of our study of cat lore this is a most interesting symbolism, for while the lion is linked indissolubly with the Sun, its smaller cousin, the cat, is always linked with the Moon. In occult terms, it is as though the cat is the soul (anima) to the lion spirit (spiritus). The astrological link with the Sun is expressed in the most surprising occult and arcane symbols – for example, we find a lion's head in the centre of the part-zodiacs on the fountain in the Piazza Signoria of Florence. This lion's head is not to be confused with the lion of zodiacal Leo. It is the lion of the Sun, visualized at the centre of the cosmos, with the twelve signs of the zodiac wheeling around it. Not far from the Signoria is the curved Via Torta, a road which marks out where the ancient Roman amphitheatre used to be. The palatial entrance to number 14 Via Torta is guarded by a pair of feline heads (Plate 15) which act as capitals for the imposing entrance. These are probably intended to be lionesses, and they have a very ancient ancestry as gate guardians for we find a lioness on guard above the cyclopaean entrance to Mycenae in the Peloponnese. We may be fairly sure that the notion behind adopting these creatures as guardians is derived from their link with the Sun, for the creative nature of the solar body has always been regarded by occultists as a most powerful amuletic device against evil. The importance of the Sun (and therefore of the associate lion) in Florentine symbolism may be seen from the curious fact that the two most important mediaeval marble zodiacs in Europe are found in this city – one in the Baptistry of St John, the other in San Miniato al Monte on the hill just outside the old gates of Florence – and each of these has a Sun symbol at the centre of the zodiacal circle. Again and again in occultism, as in Christian symbolism, we find symbols

Fig. 24   Lion and lioness as symbols of spirit and soul united. From the alchemical text De Lapide Philosophico *by Lambsprinck, 1677*

expressing the notion that the Sun is a power for good and the Moon a planet of evil, linked with demons.

It is often very easy to confuse the lion with the cat in symbolic art. In her book on the archetypal cat, Patricia Dale-Green makes the assumption that on the top of the cross at Kirk Braddan two cats support a human face (figure 25). With regard to this supposed image, she quotes Plutarch who tells us that when we find a human face between two cat-like figures, they are designed to show that the changes of the Moon are regulated by wisdom and understanding. In fact, the two animals are not cats but lions, and the image is a fairly traditional one relating to the story of Daniel in the lion's den, which makes the reference to Plutarch irrelevant.

Fig. 25   The head of the cross at Kirk Braddan, which has been claimed to be a source of feline imagery, but which is in fact linked with the story of Daniel in the lion's den. After the drawing in P. M. C. Kermode's The Manx Archaeological Survey *(1909–1918)*

Generally speaking the lion in mediaeval symbolism has a meaning dependent upon context and even locality. In the mediaeval regions where Venice predominated, the image of the lion is almost always a reference to the heraldic animal of the maritime island-city. In many cases, as for example in Padua, the Venetian lion looks towards the rising sun, towards the east from which so much of the wealth which made the city great was derived. The lion in almost all regions is also the emblematic symbol of St Mark (from which the Venetian lion was ultimately derived), itself having origins traced to the zodiacal Leo which was a lion in ancient Babylonian and Egyptian symbolism. Sometimes the lion is lifted straight out of the fables and travel books, as, for example, the lion in the capital of the pillar of the raised Palazzo della Ragione in Bergamo, which stands over one of the most fascinating zodiacal clocks in Europe. This thirteenth-century lion has nothing to do with the zodiac, however, but merely portrays an incident from a folk tale. But since in esoteric imagery, the lion is almost always in some way linked with the Sun, and with that inner representative of the sun in the human body, which is the heart, it is no wonder that the heart of man is guarded by the zodiacal lion in the traditional image of zodiacal man.

In view of this it is not surprising that the lion of Leo pops up in various disguises in alchemy, especially as the adepts of the art often described twelve alchemical processes which corresponded in one way or another with the twelve signs of the zodiac. Also, the mediaeval symbolism of the lion was incorporated into alchemical symbolism. The lion of the mediaeval virtues which entered into the Tarot tradition as the 'Strength' card plays its part in alchemical symbolism; but more frequently the lion was adapted as a symbol of the element of Fire. We may trace this strain of symbolism to the fact that the four elements were often represented in terms of the four fixed signs of the zodiac, which were Taurus, Leo, Scorpio and Aquarius. The corresponding images for these were the Bull, the Lion, the Eagle and the Human Being or the Human Face: these appear in literally thousands of occult symbolic forms throughout the whole period of alchemical and hermetic symbolism. Again, because of the link with the element of Fire, the lion is sometimes used to symbolize the human temperament of the Choleric (the fire type). We see this symbolism delightfully set out in the graphics of Simon Vostre's *Book of Hours* of 1502, in which (top left) the Lion represents the Fire temperament and (top right) the monkey represents the Air or Sanguine temperament (figure 26).

Fig. 26   Emblems of the four temperaments around the image of Death (clockwise from top left, Choleric, Sanguine, Melancholic and Phlegmatic). From Simon Vostre's Book of Hours, *1502*

In alchemy, however, the Lion was sometimes drawn as though it were a pussy cat. This in itself was probably not due so much to any inability of the woodcutters or artists, as to the alchemists' wish to point to the fact that the cat, as much as the lion, was linked in the secret art with heat. After all, the Sekhmet of the Egyptians (from which alchemy is said to have derived) was among other things a goddess of fire.

There is a very interesting cat-head to the left of the rebus on the title page of one of the most influential alchemical texts of the seventeenth century, the *De Lapide Philosophico*, of Lambsprinck, in which we have already noted the use of alchemical lion symbolism (figure 27). We can see its head emerging from the cave in the hill on which sits the solar king: the ray of the central star bears the number 2, and the sigil for Jupiter points towards both the king and the cat. This cat is derived from the 'leonine' tradition, of course, yet its placing in such an important occult figure makes it worthy of some comment. Below the cat we can see a dragon belching forth flames, and above it is the king, with a solar halo, above which a hand-held torch protrudes. The newt-like salamander and the Sun marked 'Anima' on this side of the design leave us in no doubt that this is the solar or 'fire' side of the human being.

The human being is schematically drawn as a biped inverted triangle,

Fig. 27   Title page of Lambsprinck's De Lapide Philosophico *of 1677, with feline lion below the personification of the Sun (left of central diagram)*

with one leg on the waves of the lunar side of the design and the other leg on the earth. The inner life of the human is symbolically represented in the inverted triangle marked 'Anima', 'Spiritus' and 'Corpus' – alchemical names for Soul, Spirit and Body, the hermetic names for the modern occult concepts of Thinking, Feeling and Willing. The inverted triangle is echoed in the human face at the centre, from which radiate the seven planetary rays, each linked with an alchemical process. What is the significance of the cat's head within the framework of these curious symbols?

The cat is emerging from the earth – that in itself is not without significance. The dragon below it is also emerging from the earth. We may take it that the symbolism is concerned with expressing the idea that both the dragon and the cat are linked with what we would now call the 'subconscious' realm, with those elements in man which are hidden from the light of consciousness. The flames of the dragon are fearsome, while the flames around the cat are probably merely a throwback to the lion's mane. Whatever their origin, they are not so fearsome as those of the dragon, and they are not emitted from within its body, but cling as it were to the outside of its body. These flames are transformed into a halo around the king who sits above the cat: they are now entirely external, and symbolic of a spiritual force. In the torch above they are being used to give light to the world, while the flames which proceed from the salamander above are entirely spiritual, for the salamander is said to live in a secret hidden fire, which is why the salamander or fire-newt is invisible to the ordinary vision of man.

In this series of five fire-symbols we may trace a progression of symbolism, from the inner fires of the subconscious dragon up to the hidden and transformed spiritual fires of the salamander. Alchemy itself is involved with this 'spiritualization' of inner qualities, with what we might call the taming of the inner dragon. Our cat marks the second stage of this progression, and the cat's head, wreathed in a 'mane' of external flames, says a great deal about the nature of the inner man. The cat is one of the few creatures which has been 'tamed' and domesticated. In its untamed nature it is a lion. The cat has been transformed by human love, so that the symbolism of the design implies that before the powerful energies of the dragon can be used by the human intent on developing his inner world, he must transform the inner dragon by love. One of the messages in this rebus is that the whole secret of the alchemical art rests on love. We might indeed see the alchemical image

Fig. 28   The Tarot designs of the 'Juggler' and the 'Fool', from Court de Gebelin's Le Monde Primitif, *1781. Note that the fool is being attacked by a cat*

of the lion swallowing the Sun as a profound symbol of the relationship between the untamed dragon and the cat which dwells unheeded within all men. Is it not one of the most profound commentaries on the nature of the cat that it has been adopted by all important occultists as a symbol of the inner sun, as well as the most abiding symbol of the moon?

If we turn to some of the occult images which are derived from the mediaeval lore we find that one of the pictures of the set of divinatory cards of the Tarot pack depicted a cat. The illustration of the 'Fool' and the 'Juggler' cards reproduced by Court de Gebelin in 1781 (figure 28) show the Fool with a lynx-like cat leaping at his legs. In the modern cards – which is to say, in those printed after the eighteenth century – the cat has been changed into a dog (figure 29), but the reasons for this need not concern us here. The Court de Gebelin drawings are slight things in themselves, scarcely works of art, yet even so they exhibit very interesting occult strains in which the symbolism of the cat plays an important role.

In a specifically occult sense, the Fool and Juggler cards in de

Fig. 29   The Tarot design of the 'Fool' from an early nineteenth-century version of the Marseilles pack. Note that the fool is being attacked by a dog

Gebelin's drawing of figure 28 are related. The Fool shows a man who is setting off on the spiritual journey: it is said that in the sack which he carries over his back are many treasures (the 'inner treasures' of course), but he is ignorant of their true worth. In the following card of the Tarot sequence (the Juggler), the man has taken out these objects and has spread them on the table. He is now the juggler, the man of real magic, who is prepared to use his treasures. The secret symbolism in these cards confirms this simple interpretation in many details. If, for example, we look at the structure of the curious sack which the man has strung over the stick on his shoulder, we observe that its lower part has been drawn in such a way as to evoke the crescent Moon. His 'inner treasure' is some-how linked with the Moon. The cat at his feet is also linked with the

Moon, as we now know from our survey of the cat in occult lore. Do we find any arcane reference to the Moon in the second card – in that card which represents a stage of spiritual development of the Fool into the Juggler? The answer is that we do, but that in this second card the Moon is harmoniously related to the Sun.

There are two very interesting symbols in the image of the Juggler. One is found in the structure of his curious hat, and the other in the symbolism of an object (or objects) on the table in front of him, which is probably intended to represent two coins. Modern occultists call these symbols 'lemniscates', but in popular use they are called 'figures of eight'. In occult symbolism, the figure of eight represents the coming together of the Sun and the Moon, which touch at a single point where their circumferences meet. In alchemical or occult terms, this union of the Sun and Moon is regarded as a symbol of the harmonious unification within the human being of the male and female principles. Those occultists and alchemists who seek to develop inner perfection in man, claim that unless the inner 'solar' and 'lunar' energies unite harmoniously, such a spiritual development cannot take place. It is for this reason that the lemniscate figure in Christian and occult art forms is used as a symbol of unity.

If we consider once more the meaning of the two cards in the light of this lemniscate symbolism, we see that the Fool card represents a one-sided man. The symbols are entirely lunar – even to the crescent form which crowns his curious hat. In the next card, however, it is as though this lunar element were balanced, and is no longer an insistent part of the card's imagery. In the Juggler the Moon is in harmonious contact with the Sun, as the coins and hat-form indicate, and the man is in a position to start that inner development which he envisaged when he started on the spiritual journey. There are other occult symbols within these two cards, but these do not concern us here: we might, however, note that the Fool's belt is decorated with four divided circles, which represent the four phases of the Moon (full, waxing, waning and gibbous), and explain why the number 4 (as well as the number 3) has been associated with the Moon in arcane symbolism. Our real interest in these two cards, however, is in the cat.

We may take it that this Tarot cat represents the lower passions associated with the Moon. This is a reasonable assumption, for the cat was linked with the Devil, and the demonic sphere has always been linked with the sphere of the Moon. It is said that the crescent horns which the demons sport are the symbol of the crescent Moon, which is their true home. Perhaps these associations explain why the cat is scratching at the man's breeches, for it is said that as soon as a human being sets out on the path of spiritual perfection, the demon world becomes deeply concerned. It has no wish to see a human soul develop itself, for in this way it loosens that soul from its own clutches. The ordinary man has no need for concern, as the demons do not openly attack him: the demons know that in time (all things being equal) his soul will come to them. But a man who consciously sets out to perfect his inner world is actually seeking to reject the demonic, and so the demons make their presence felt, often objecting vociferously.

There is clearly a relationship between the esoteric symbolism of the Tarot cat and the cat-familiar of the witches, for both are symbolic embodiments of the demonic. Yet the symbolism of the Tarot card is of a higher order than the witchcraft symbolism, and we may see that the two cards portray in a most subtle way how the cat may be used in the programme of spiritual development. There is a distinct sense in which the table behind which the Juggler stands is a transformation of the cat. This may sound absurd, but in occult terms it is not. The cat has four legs, the table has four legs. The cat is a symbol of the demons which dwell within the centre of the earth: the table is made of earthly material, and the four legs may be interpreted as representing the four elements of Earth, Air, Fire and Water. This is almost taken for granted by the Juggler, but Court de Gebelin may be forgiven for making some slight alterations to his designs in order to demonstrate this connexion between the 'demonic cat' which merely attacks the man, and the table, which is of use to the man. Note that the legs of the table are very curious indeed. In terms of the ordinary rules of perspective, it would be quite impossible for the Juggler's left foot to stand in front of the foreground table leg – yet this is precisely what it does. Why does Court de Gebelin distort so strangely the ordinary laws of space? The interesting thing is that one of the legs of the cat is also hidden – this time by the foot of the man. This is an example of the subtle symbolism to which an occultist will resort when he wishes to speak of the secret things.

The Fool has to change everything if he is to continue on his spiritual journey. He must change his hat, from an exuberant lunar device to a more calm lemniscatory symbol. The hat is symbol of his way of thinking, so we see that the card indicates that there must be a change of attitude, a change of thought on this spiritual journey. He must open up his sack, and study its secret hoard. The secrets are now spread out before him, in the light of consciousness. The sack is symbol of his inner soul life, or of his emotional life. When the sack is carried behind him, on his back, it is perhaps too close to his head, as symbol of the ordinary confusion which exists between thinking and feeling. In the Juggler's symbolism, however, the thinking is harmonious, and quite separate from the feeling, symbolized in the paraphernalia on the table. The cat is symbol of the lower nature. The Fool carries a stick, as though this were needed to constantly beat down the lower passions which seem to be attacking his sexual parts. The serene Juggler has made use of this cat – he no longer beats it, and has thrown away his big stick, holding up to the sky only a small version of the stick as though making an offering to the heavens. Perhaps the big stick has been transformed into a magic wand? By his magic, the Juggler has transformed the lower passions and made them serviceable to his needs. It is a magical table, which defies the rules of space. The demonic element within the cat has been transformed into a magical table, to become symbol of the four elements from which the entire world has been made.

There is an element of heresy in these two strange cards, for the last important heretical groups in Europe were those derived from the Gnostics of Egypt, who insisted that the earth had been created not by God but by the Devil. Everything made from the four elements had been made by the Devil, which is why earthly things had to be sloughed off and transformed, used as a vehicle for spirit. Perhaps this is the secret message carried by the cat at the feet of the Fool?

The modern card, which is technically called an 'atout' or 'arcanum', shows an ill-dressed man walking towards the right, a sack of belongings over his back and the animal following on behind (figure 29). We may see, therefore, that in the days when the Whittington story began to circulate, there was an occult tradition which linked a wanderer with a cat. Perhaps there is no accident in the fact that popular posters for Dick Whittington usually show him walking with a bundle over his shoulder, the cat at his feet? Is this a racial memory, or the accidental continuation of the same sort of survival of occult nuance which we note in certain fairytales?

The occult background to this card may throw some light on the cat. The antiquity of the Tarot cards is unknown, but there is evidence to show that they were in use in Italy as playing cards in the late fourteenth century. When they were first used for divinatory purposes no one may be sure, but by the sixteenth century there is no doubt that the Tarot pack, in a form which resembles to some extent the modern pictures, was used to foretell the future. The 'Fool' card is the only one in the series of 22 arcana which is unnumbered, and while the popular notion is that the image does indeed depict a fool, the hermetic tradition insists that this is not the case. The occult view is that the true initiate often appears to those around him to behave like a fool. This is because he has insights and knowledge which determine his actions in a way beyond the comprehension of his usual associates. The man appears to be a fool, but in reality he is a cunning wise man, disguised behind the appearance of foolhardiness. What are the symbols in the original images which indicate that the man may be regarded as an initiate? Curiously enough, one of the most outstanding symbols is the fact that he is depicted wearing one of his stockings half way down his leg. This symbolism, which has survived in a·curious form in certain modern Masonic rites, is widely used in late mediaeval art as a device to indicate that the person depicted is an initiate. The secret idea behind the stocking has been lost, yet there is no doubt that as a symbolic device it was widely used in alchemical, Rosicrucian and general occult pictures.

Where does the cat come into this arcane framework of symbols? If we take the card to be occult, rather than an exoteric design, we may see the cat within the framework of occult symbolism. It is generally taken for granted that when an animal, or some theriomorphic form, is portrayed at the foot of a person, then that creature is meant to symbolize some inner evil which has been overcome. The numerous pictures of St Michael standing over the serpentine Satan, the images of St Margaret standing over the dragon, the religious icon which shows the Virgin standing on the Moon, all point to the idea of a human being triumphing over some inner vice or evil. The story tells how St Michael overcomes the Devil, and fights with him for the souls of the newly dead. The Christian mythology tells how the virgin Margaret was swallowed by the dragon while in prison, and how, when she made the sign of the cross, the belly of the dragon split open. Such stories, which have resulted in thousands of illustrations and icons, may be seen as arcane references to initiation rites which permit humans to experience the higher world, remember what they have seen and heard, and then return to the ordinary life with a part of their inner being 'sloughed off' in a demonic or animal form.

If this is the case with the unnumbered arcanum of the Tarot pack,

what does the cat symbolize? What has the initiate sloughed off into the
form of a cat, which follows him during his journeys through the earth?
We may look at this symbolism in a very simple way, and recall that in
the late mediaeval period the cat – especially the black cat – was linked
with the Devil. If this were the appropriate way of interpreting the Fool
card, then we might see it as an image of an initiate who had sloughed
off the darker part of himself, as a result of which he is now inwardly
pure. In such an interpretation there is an obvious link with the Devil-
slaying of St Michael. However, there is also a less obvious link with the
lunar crescent over which the Virgin Mary stands, for the cat has been
associated with the Moon since very ancient times. Such a way of interpreting the Tarot cat is strictly in accordance with the occult symbolism,
for in some Tarot images it is clear that the cat is not very friendly to the
man, and is indeed attacking his legs. It is just so with many of the
Michael pictures, for the Devil is not 'killed', but merely put in his place,
at the feet of man. While the initiate has overcome the lower part of his

Fig. 30   The 'Devil' of the Kuykendall Tarot of the Cat People. Design copyright Karen
Kuykendall: reproduced with the permission of the artist

Fig. 31   Witches raising a storm by magical means. The skull on the pole held by the warlock in the foreground is almost certainly that of a cat. From the seventeenth-century edition of Olaus Magnus' Historia Gentium Septentrionalibus

being, the Devil which is in every man, he has not killed the creature, and must be constantly on his guard to ensure that the demon does not regain its old ascendancy.

There is one remarkable set of modern Tarot cards which owes its inspiration almost entirely to the lore of the cat. This set, designed by Karen Kuykendall over a period of two years and published in 1985, incorporates feline imagery into the major and minor arcana of the Tarot pack in a most ingenious way. The symbolism of the *Tarot of the Cat People* (Plate 16) is not entirely 'occult', for it combines elements of anthropological origin with what may only be described as elements of science fiction. Each of the five occult divisions of the pack (the Major Arcana and the Swords, Wands, Cups and Pentacles of the Minor Arcana, which correspond in the occult tradition to the five elements of the alchemists) are related to 'Five Kingdoms', named respectively Vapala (of the 'Sky People'), Thnossis (of the 'Fire People'), Twahihic (of the 'Sand People'), the Azhengir (of the 'Salt People') and the Kahulawe (of the 'Rock People'). The symbolism of the cat is interwoven into the legends and beliefs of these regions and figures on each of the Tarot cards. In particular the symbolism of the Moon Card (Plate 16), with the new crescent of the moon growing as it were from the mouth of the lunar goddess, the tail of the feline echoing the crescent of the Moon, is linked with the occult tradition of symbolism. Equally, the three-pointed dart on the head of the lance in the hand of the goddess is of an occult derivation as it is intended no doubt to recall the triple goddess of the Moon whom the ancients called Hecate and who was the source of the numerological connexion between the figure 3 and the Moon. In a similar fashion, the two demons of the original Devil Card are trans-

Fig. 32   The design for 'The Chariot' from Kuykendall's Tarot of the Cat People. *Design copyright Karen Kuykendall: reproduced by permission of the artist*

formed by Kuykendall into two felines which we presume to be demonic familiars (figure 30). The cat-headed wand in the hand of this Teutonic devil also recalls the ancient occult tradition, which we see figured in a woodcut illustrating witches and warlocks causing shipwrecks with their magical practices. In this woodcut, the seated warlock in the foreground is holding a staff on which has been impaled the skull of a small animal, as may be seen in the detail of figure 31. It is likely that this skull is from the body of a cat, for as we shall see in chapter 7 it was widely believed that cats were indeed sacrificed by witches and used in the storm-raising black magic of witch covens.

Other cards from the Kuykendall pack are less obviously linked with the occult tradition, and depend for their symbolism on the mythology woven around the Five Kingdoms. For example, 'The Chariot' card (figure 32) portrays the two felines which draw the chariot as virtually identical twins, while in the occult symbolism of the original card it is important that they represent 'dualism', so they are of different colours and pull in opposing directions. The sixteenth atout, 'The Tower' is again involved with private symbolism. What we see in the Kuykendall pack is a huge stone cat being struck by a thunder-flash, with a man, woman and cat falling from its higher levels. The original card shows a tower with men falling from it, and with lightning striking the fabric: the design is sometimes called 'The House of God', which was one of the mediaeval names for a hospital. The traditional imagery appears to be derived from a mediaeval account of the journey made by Christ into Egypt, when those pagan idols which would not bow down to him fell to ruin from their high places on the temple. One of the occult-derived images on the façade of Amiens cathedral tells this story in graphic detail. The arcane references of the ancient Tarot are lost in the Kuykendall pack, yet new lines of occult symbolism are introduced, for the explanatory booklet makes it clear that the auras around the falling people and cat are intended to show that they are protected from being damaged as they fall, while the card as a whole represents in the divinatory interpretation a 'complete and sudden change' for those concerned, since, for all their protective auras, people are not as adept as the cat at landing from great heights.

While touching upon the significance of the cat in connexion with the Tarot card of the Fool, we might note a related occult interpretation of a catskin in the curious and emblematic paintings of the fifteenth-century artist Hieronymus Bosch, who appears to have worked at times

Fig. 33 *'The Prodigal Son' by Hieronymus Bosch. Collection of the Museum Boymans-van Beuningen, Rotterdam. The symbolism of the catskin attached to the pedlar's basket has intrigued many art historians*

for a group of heretics concerned with secret symbolism. The 'wanderer' in the 'Prodigal Son' (figure 33) bears several signs of initiation – note, for example, the handkerchief or garter tied around his left leg. The bundle on his back, and the presence of the animal behind him evoke some of the arcane symbolism of the Fool card, though the painting is nominally intended to illustrate the Biblical parable in Luke 15, 11–32. Bosch is no doubt drawing a parallel between this parable and the life of the initiate, who gives up all worldly wealth for the riches of spirit, and eventually returns to his Father's house (which is heaven) the wiser for his experience on earth. What is of immediate interest to us, however, is the occult significance of the catskin which is tied beneath the spoon on the pannier which the prodigal carries on his back. The art historian Wertheim Aymes has given a very able interpretation of this picture from a point of view of secret symbolism. In special regard to the catskin, he emphasizes the old idea of the cat as a creature of change, 'drowsy by day, doubly active by night'. The cat is a creature of phase in its moods also, alternating periods of contented calm with emotional or passionate outbursts. Aymes sees in this alternation of phases a good reason why the Egyptian goddess of the magic of love (Bastet) should be depicted with the head of a cat. He sees the catskin as a symbol of the death of the passionate experiences connected with love. In other words, this catskin has much the same magical importance within the framework of secret symbolism with which Bosch's 'Prodigal Son' abounds as the 'dead' or 'vanquished' animals in other forms of art. The catskin is a relic of some vice or passion which has been rejected from the spiritual life of the prodigal.

The art historian D. Bax, who tends to treat most of Bosch's symbols as though they were of a literary nature, points out that the catskins of the pedlar appear in several other paintings, and that catskins were articles which genuine pedlars attached to their pack-baskets. Even so, he does trace a symbolic significance in the skins on the grounds that they evoke the Dutch word *katsjager* (cat-hunter), one of the names used for a woman-chaser. However, having made this point, Bax appears to reject the interpretation as scarcely valid in terms of the picture, for the pedlar is not a woman-chaser, but one apparently beset by the difficulties of poverty.

As an alternative reading, he points out that the word *kattevel* (catskin) is used to denote a purse made from such skin, and he quotes one or two literary sources in support of this. The interpretation is taken a step further when Bax indicates that the skin is that of a flayed cat, and that the Dutch word *stropen* had by the fifteenth century acquired the figurative meaning of 'fleecing' or stealing. From this we may interpret the catskin as a symbol that the pedlar's purse had been stolen. The interpretation does not appear to follow the methods of symbolism employed in sixteenth-century art, however, and the significance of the catskin may be seen in more simple terms as a reference to the very word which Bax rejects – the 'woman-chaser' (*katsjager*). If this painting is concerned with esoteric symbolism (a notion which Bax appears to reject, yet one which many occultists propose), then we may interpret the catskin in much the same way as we interpret the hidden things in the sack of the Tarot 'Fool'. That is to say that the catskin represents a treasure unrecognized by the pedlar. What is the value in a *katsjager*? The pursuit of women is nothing more than the debased pursuit of the heavenly woman, of the anima – the pursuit indeed of the Queen of Heaven. In pagan times this Queen of Heaven was the lunar Isis, or even the goddess Bastet, but within the Christian framework it is the Virgin Mary. The time will come when the prodigal son will recognize the value of the thing he carries on his back, for it is symbol of his link with the heavenly stars.

Bosch painted several demonic felines, and we shall examine something of the significance of these later (page 149), but at this point we should observe a most distinctive cat in one of the most lovely of all his panels – the internal wing of his triptych 'The Garden of Heavenly Delights', also in the Prado. To the left of the charmingly 'innocent' picture of Adam and Eve is a tree, at the foot of which is a cat carrying what appears to be a dead rat (Plate 17). It is interesting to note that this panel is divided into two distinct areas. The division is made by the woodlands and foliage behind the figures of Adam, Eve and God. The upper part, which centres upon the fountain with its strange landscape, littered with a number of animals which are definable, such as the elephant, the giraffe, the unicorn, and a certain number which are not identifiable, almost certainly relates to the Heavenly Paradise. The lower part centres on Adam and Eve, and is populated by animals and birds which can only be described as demonic. The three-headed bird is drinking from a dark pool, which appears to be the shadow image of the heavenly pool of the upper register, from which unicorns drink. Nothing is quite what it first appears to be in this picture. To the right of the fountain is a rock on which are two animals: the lower saurian forms a moustache and chin from the rock, while the shelled creature makes a large eye. The fountain itself is almost anthropomorphic, and certain of the creatures in the heavenly upper part are sinister or peculiar. Thus, there is a Daliesque quality in the picture which disturbs our consciousness, and encourages us to look at the details with inquiring eyes.

On examination, the cat appears not to be quite so feline as we might have thought. The tail does not arch from the body in quite the way it should, nor are the protruding teeth quite the dentures of a cat. The front paws at least are more like the talons of a demon than those proper to a cat. Is it a cat at all, one wonders? Even if we are certain that it is meant

Fig. 34   'Adam and Eve'. Engraving by Albrecht Dürer, 1504. The cat in the foreground, apparently unaware of the mouse by Adam's right foot, is a symbol of the choleric nature (as yet unawakened, because the Fall has not taken place), while the animals behind Eve represent the three remaining temperaments

to represent a cat, we must still ask ourselves what it is intended to symbolize? If we relate it to the idea of the 'cat and mouse' symbolism that may be observed in the Dürer print (figure 34), and which is discussed on pages 184–5, we might see the cat and rat as a symbolic prevision of the coming Fall of Man. This is perhaps why Bosch has placed his demonic feline at the foot of the tree, which bears that tempting fruit, half-strawberry, half-grape. Is this cat then a symbol of the tempting Satan, carrying away his victim which is man? If this suggested interpretation seems reasonable, then we might return to the notion of the Dutch word *katsjager* to which Bax refers. The 'hunter cat' who is at the same time a 'hunter of women', makes very good symbolic sense in this context, for according to the Bible, Satan chose to persuade the first woman to eat of the fruit: he was the original 'woman chaser'. The symbolism takes on a deeper level of meaning in view of the fact that this Satan carries his victim in his mouth, reminding us that Eve sinned by taking the forbidden fruit into her own mouth.

Bosch painted the cat within symbolic contexts fairly often, and in some cases it is clear that the intention is to convey a meaning linked with what we might call the 'debasement of the goddess' – the symbolism of heavenly Bastet reduced to a demonic level. In the superb painting of the 'Seven Deadly Sins', we see a cat introduced into the section dealing with the sin of pride ('Superbia', in Latin, as may be seen from the word at the bottom of the detail in Plate 18). The standard mediaeval symbolism shows a woman looking at herself in the mirror, which is being held in the talons of a demon. Almost every detail in the picture reflects an aspect of this sin of pride, including the small grey cat which may be seen through the open doorway to the right. Perhaps the cat was adopted here as a symbol of pride because the sin arises from vision (from how one sees oneself); but in a general sense we may be sure that in the late mediaeval tradition the cat figures as symbol both of pride and of the faculty of sight, the latter no doubt arising from its extraordinary eyes. This cat is especially important within the framework of the entire picture, for the panel is organized as a circle, the seven deadly sins painted in sequence in its seven segments and the central circle something like an eye, with an image of the resurrected Christ and the Latin inscription, 'Cave, Cave, Deus Videt' (Beware, beware, God sees). With this central symbolism of the seeing god, the picture of a woman looking into a mirror has a double meaning, for it indicates that while she is herself filled with pride, and thus falls into the grasp of the demons, God cannot feel any pride for what he sees in the mirror of the world below. The cat, as a demoted goddess, is therefore a particularly poignant arcane symbol, representative of what the world has come to through the propensity of man to sin. It is easy to see why the melancholic Spanish King Philip II kept this panel in his bedroom as an object lesson in morality.

In passing, we could note an unconventional use of feline symbolism which still remains within the demonic tradition. The cat as symbol appears to have interested Philip II, for there are records of his attending a recital of a cat organ in Brussels in 1549. This curious organ was played not on air pipes but on the squeals of cats. Although no picture of the cat organ which Philip listened to appears to have survived, an engraving of the next century, from Schott's *Magiae Universalis* (figure 35) illustrates

Fig. 35   Cat-organ – an engraved illustration to Part II, Book VI, 'Felium Musicam Exhibere', of Gaspar Schott's Magiae Universalis, *1657*

the principle. In place of the usual wind-pipes the organ had twenty caged cats with cords fastened to their tails. When a key of the organ was pressed, a corresponding tail was pulled, and the cat made a sound. It is said that the 1549 entertainment involved a bear playing the keys, but how this creature was cajoled into hitting the correct sequence is anybody's guess.

Although it would be fatuous to read too deeply into the arcane symbolism of such a device, which was intended mainly for 'amusement', it is quite possible that it represented a serious attempt to invent a demonic music. In the late mediaeval period it was firmly believed that earthly music was nothing more than a shadow of the celestial music, the so-called 'Music of the Spheres', which could be heard by adepts and wise men only. This theory of heavenly music was based on the idea that the ratios of the distances of the planetary spheres was such that they corresponded to the ratios upon which earthly music rested. It was held that the music of the heavenly bodies sounded in harmony as these bodies circled in their respective spheres. In the early seventeenth century the great astronomer Kepler amended this ancient theory to adapt it to the heliocentric system which was by then gaining wide acceptance. His notion was that the music of the spheres was linked not with distances but with the diurnal angles of the planets in their heavenly motions, which he showed demonstrated a complete system of musical intervals. The idea that earthly music was a shadowy reflection of a superior planetary music was therefore widely spread at the time when the cat-organ was developed. In these days it was almost taken for granted that the cat was an agent of the Devil, so we must assume that those who played this curious instrument were intent on making a new kind of music – one which found a correspondence with the infernal regions, rather than with the heavenly realms. Figure 36, which illustrates a similar 'cat-organ' with demonic accompaniment, would appear to support this thesis.

In a sixteenth-century fresco in the so-called 'Chamber of Rhetoric' in Antwerp a jester holds a cat in his hand and proclaims, 'I have found her.' Has he found the inner meaning of the cat? After seeing how deeply the 'hellish tomcat' symbolism is linked with the diabolic in

Fig. 36   Cat-organ with demonic choir. From a seventeenth-century print by Franz van der Wyngaert

fifteenth-and sixteenth-century art, it may appear absurd to interpret the cat as symbol of the highest potential within man, of the ability to commune with the anima or with the religious symbol of the anima, the Virgin Mary. However, the cat is undoubtedly a complex symbol, and quite capable of representing the two extremes of hell and heaven: indeed, it may be in this symbolism of extremes that the power of cat symbolism rests. Friedmann, in his *A Bestiary for St Jerome*, points out that the domestic cat represents the attributes of family and forebears of the Virgin, of the 'plain, unassuming Judaean maiden who was destined to be transformed and elevated by divine choice.' The real power of Bosch's use of the cat as symbol is that it rests upon the notion of 'debasement'. The unrecognized treasure of the catskin – itself nothing more than the rejected surface of a once living thing – is really a treasure of great price: the hellish is really the heavenly.

Fig. 37   Detail of an engraving 'The Feast of Fools' by H. Cock, after a drawing by Brueghel the Elder

In one of the engravings after Brueghel the Elder, we see a fool dancing with a cat on his shoulders (figure 37), while in an engraving after Bosch a cat is seen in the folds of the hood of a merrymaker who is in a mussel-shell. In esoteric terms any symbol worn on the head (such as a hat) indicates the relationship which the wearer has with the spiritual realm above. A reveller involved in the unlikely symbolism of carrying a cat on his head no doubt fails to understand the true significance of the cat, as the virgin Queen of Heaven.

As we shall see, the cat suffered personally at the hands of the witch-craft mongers, mainly because most were suspected of being 'imps' and therefore demons in disguise. This attitude to the feline race is reflected in art and literature: for every painting which shows the cat as a valued pet there must be a dozen images of the cat as a symbol of evil, or being maltreated.

In the upper corridors of the Uffizi in Florence hang a series of sixteenth-century tapestries dealing with the passion of Christ. The first of these depicts the Last Supper with a short text from Matthew 26, 23 – 'He that dippeth his hand with me in the dish, the same shall betray me.' In the foreground of this huge tapestry is a cat, which is being handed a sop by one of the disciples, whom we presume to be Judas. In the Gospel of John (13, 27) it is said that immediately after Judas had taken the sop that Jesus gave to him Satan entered into him. Here, in a most sophisticated art-form, we see the cat as emblem of the Devil, to whom Judas is paying homage by donating to the creature the bread which was to become the symbol of the body of Christ (Plate 3). The same symbolism appears in several Renaissance and post-Renaissance pictures. A fresco of the 'Last Supper' by Luini (figure 38) in Santa Maria degli Angeli, Lugano, has a detail showing Judas clutching (perhaps a little too early, as the Last Supper is not yet over) his bag of silver, with a striped cat at his feet. In her excellent book *The Cult of the Cat*, Patricia Dale-Green actually calls the feline of this symbolism the 'Judas Cat'.

After the fifteenth century, the cat enters more and more into Christian art as a symbol of evil, which makes its presence at the foot of Christ in Andrea Boscoli's 'Marriage at Cana', all the more remarkable. What is the symbolism behind this strange image? Above the head of the cat flies a bird, which is fluttering at the end of a string held in the hands of a young boy. The cat is backing away from the attack of a dog, while Christ sits quietly, seemingly oblivious to the noise of the barking. If this cat is meant to symbolize an evil power, it is difficult to see what it is doing

Fig. 38   The Judas Cat – detail of the fresco of The Last Supper *by Bernadino Luini, in Santa Maria degli Angeli, Lugano*

sheltering in the robes of Christ. The captive bird hovering over the cat might recall images of the Dove, sometimes attached by filigrees of gold to the hand of God as it hovers over the head of Christ in the baptism at Jordan. The cat is being beset by a dog in much the same way as Christ will be beset by the soldiers and priests prior to his crucifixion. Is this detail intended to symbolize the Baptism and the Passion, between which the marriage at Cana is a sort of midpoint, with Christ, already baptized, about to perform his miracle of changing water to wine? This miracle was often seen as a prefiguring of the changing of wine to blood, as was first done at the Last Supper, itself the prototype for the Mass. If this interpretation is correct, then we are beginning to see the cat redeemed as a Christian symbol, for it is identified with the suffering of Christ. Perhaps this interpretation alone will explain why it seems to seek the robe of Christ for safety, as it cowers away from the dog.

'Never drown or beat a cat, for the Devil will get you,' claims one of the much quoted popular adages in early books on felines; yet the sad story of cruelty to the feline race suggests that the belief is not deep rooted. The saying springs from the notion that the cat is a sacred animal – just like the saying, recorded in *Folk Beliefs of the Southern Negro* by Puckeld, that while a cat has nine lives, you need take only one of these and the cat will haunt you. How can there be such a wide divergence between beliefs and practices? Is the divergence merely yet another sign of the devolution of the cat from a goddess to an imp? Were all the popular sayings derived from the folk wisdom which regards the cat as a superior being, a goddess, while the cruel or rejective behaviour is derived from the image of the witch-imp of more immediate and familiar history?

In the Bargello Museum is an early sixteenth-century enamel by Couly Nouailher of Limoges, part of a series on twelve related themes, which shows a pair of cupids belabouring a cat with a stick (Plate 19). This cat appears to be of the domesticated kind, but it stands in almost an heraldic position on a mound, as though it were some sacrificial beast. The two cupids seem to be beating the unfortunate animal with great gusto. The significance of this enamel, which was almost certainly copied from an engraving, is something of a puzzle – even the French inscription around the edge of the design is not very clear: LA BATAHE DV CHAT, which presumably means something like 'The Beating of the Cat'. We may be sure that the symbolism of this design would be understood by the person who commissioned it, or the engraving from which it was painted, but we ourselves may only speculate upon its meaning. Is the cat still the Devil, who must be beaten? One finds numerous witchcraft engravings and pictures of the Devil in the form of a goat, standing on a hillock in imitation of the Easter lamb, who is Christ. The stance of the cat recalls somewhat this 'Agnus Dei' stance, and reminds us that the Agnus Dei was the official badge or emblem of the Templars. The Lamb of God, standing on a hill or altar, sometimes devoid of the cross which it carries in the crook of its raised front leg, often appears in heraldic and occult images, as, for example, in the family arms claimed by the alchemist Lambsprinck, where it appears on both crest and shield, and where, of course, it is intended mainly as a play on the author's name. Indeed, the heraldic pose of the enamel cat, and even the fact that it is a white cat, recalls most convincingly the numerous images of the Agnus Dei which is the standard Christian symbol for the Easter, or Paschal, lamb. Is this, then, a mocking image of the opposite power to Christ, the Anti-Christ?

The enamel is almost certainly emblematic, but the scene it depicts is unfortunately not far removed from reality, for there are many records of almost ritualistic cat-beating and cruelties of a like nature. In the eighteenth century a 'sport' was reported in Kelso in which a cat was placed in a barrel full of soot, and then suspended on a cross-beam between two high poles. A prescribed number of whip-men then took to horseback and struck at the barrel with mallets and sticks, until it broke free from its metal hoops and disintegrated, allowing cat and soot to fall. The cat was then further maltreated to death. The beating ritual is old, but the use of a cat-barrel is perhaps regional, and smacks of witchcraft. The normal method for killing witches in Scotland (apart from the official burning) was to put the unfortunates in a barrel filled with burning tar, and to roll them down the local hill. There are many mute testimonies – usually called witch-stones – to where such charred remains were left after these ghastly murders: an accessible one is opposite the police station in Elgin.

The sacrificial lamb, or Agnus Dei, sometimes spills its blood into the chalice, as symbol of the sacrifice of Christ. Even this sacred notion was debased in the demonic symbolism of the cat, for feline blood took on a deep significance in magical practices associated with witchcraft.

Cat's blood was regarded as having magical properties. This probably explains why some of the grimoires insist on the slaughter of a cat as a necessary prelude to black magical praxes. Could the earthenware pot in front of the cats in the Goya etching of figure 2, and in the print of witches by Baldung Grien in figure 39 be there as symbol of the blood of the cat used in the preparation of a flying salve? Behind the pot we may see the trussed hind legs of an animal (perhaps a cat) which is probably intended to symbolize just such a blood sacrifice. In his book on monsters, Martin Weinrich informs us that there was an epileptic in Warsaw who drank a cat's blood and as a result began to mew, to move like a cat, and to catch mice. Such stories originated in the days when it was believed that drinking the blood of an executed criminal was likely to result in the person being invested with the same evil tendencies. The idea was an old one (even though the occult principle of blood was generally recognized to be especially powerful) and was really only an expression of the law of 'sympathy', in which like attracts like. One of the opposite laws was that of 'antipathy', which resulted in certain created things having an aversion to each other. Thus Bartholinus, in his *De arcanis medicorum* of 1673, maintains that the well-known 'antipathy'

Fig. 39   Detail of witches with cat familiar and a bowl of flying salve, from Baldung Grien's two-colour print Die Hexen, *1510 (see Plate 21). Some of the recipes for flying salve include the blood of cats*

between cats and mice arose from occult principles, and maintained that if a granary were to be sprinkled with the ashes of cremated cats, mice would not enter. Bartholinus was deeply interested in arcane matters, and so we might well expect him to publish the old notions in his new books; but we could well be surprised to find such a man as Robert Boyle (1627–91) regarding the ear of the cat as being possessed of occult virtue, yet he followed the seventeenth-century occultist Robert Fludd in the belief that a pain in a human being might be transferred to a cat if the patient put his finger in the cat's ear. The idea that certain illnesses or diseases might be transferred to animals was fairly common in the seventeenth and eighteenth centuries, however: for example, ague and gout might be 'given' to a dog. Sometimes the cure was done by what we would now call 'transfusion', for Boyle records the case of how a madman was cured by mingling into his bloodstream the blood from a calf.

Cruelty to cats was not merely a Christian theme, however. It occurs again and again in paintings which predominate in non-symbolic social themes. Shortly after the time that Hogarth had painted the famous 'cockney cat' in his portrait of the Graham children in 1742, he began to occupy himself with the series of 'Stages of Cruelty' drawings and engravings which shows numerous indignities inflicted upon cats, as well as other animals. The first of these shows a cat, fitted with inadequate balloon wings, being thrown from a dormer window. Immediately below is the most famous of all 'cat cruelty' details from Hogarth's prints, showing two cats tied together and slung over a post in such a way that they would fight, and eventually maul each other. The cruelty is not reserved to human hands – in the foreground a cat is being savagely attacked by a dog, its entrails already visible. These awful details, part of the scene-building for the story of the fall of Tom Nero to the gallows, are not strictly speaking arcane, even though there is both hidden political satire and even direct symbolism within the picaresque journalism of the print (for example, the boy attempting to rescue the dog is a portrait of the future King George III). What is important about

Fig. 40   Detail of **The First Stage of Cruelty** *by Hogarth, showing boys laughing at two kittens who have been compelled to fight by being slung over a post*

Hogarth's work is that it broke into a new field of popular image-making, in which many of the old symbols – rendered sacrosanct by repeated use in Christian art – were presented in a new light. In this series the cat is no longer 'demonic' but the 'victim'. It was about this time, in the mid-eighteenth century, that the idea of the witch as victim was beginning to take root in our culture's intellectual life. The century saw the last trial for witchcraft, and the cat was eventually redeemed from its role as demonic familiar in all but the most die-hard of communities. There is a world of history between the woodcut of figure 39 and the engraving of figure 40.

We should not imagine that Hogarth alone regenerated the image of the cat, for there was a general move towards the pictorial journalism of which he was the finest representative. Even so the variety of feline references and symbols which he employed in many of his engravings illustrates the new attitude to cats (and indeed to animals in general) which developed in the eighteenth century as part of the liberation from the diabolic element of Christian thought.

Hogarth often worked by 'contrast', so that he would sometimes compare the conditions in 'before and after' stages of the decline of a personality, or he would produce two separate engravings which show the rise of one party and the decline of another. For example, in the before and after stages of the 'Harlot's Progress', we see the mistress of the rich Jew throwing a fit in front of her sugar daddy in order to hide her infidelity with a young lover, who is sneaking out of the room unseen by the Jew. In the foreground a monkey is scurrying away in terror at her anger. Now this monkey has a dual symbolic purpose – it is designed to show the expensive taste and spendthrift ways to which she has become accustomed (monkeys were very expensive exotic pets in the eighteenth century), and it is also a reference to her older lover, for the monkey was often used as a symbol of Jewry. Another engraving shows her decline after she has been dispensed with by the rich Jew. She is now the harlot of highwaymen, and on the point of being arrested. In the foreground is a pet cat. Were this cat seen in isolation, it would have no particular significance (though the scurrilous nature of the print is suggested by the pose of the cat, which appears to be presenting itself). However, when it is seen as the degenerate counterpart of the monkey, the cat's deeper significance immediately becomes clear. She can no longer afford expensive tastes – from the exotic she has fallen to the plebeian. Inevitably, there are also undertones of the 'witch familiar' in such a set-

*Fig. 41   Cat falling down a Chimney. In this print by Hogarth, the Idle Apprentice is in
bed with a prostitute, and they are so charged with guilt that they turn in horror when
a cat falls down the chimney. The symbolism used by Hogarth points to a double
meaning in the word 'cat', for this was one of the common names for a prostitute in the
eighteenth century – the prostitute is as much involved in a 'fall' from grace as is the
Idle Apprentice*

ting – Moll is no longer pretending to be a lady of quality, as when she
was living with the Jew; she is the consort of highwaymen, falling into
demonic temptation. The social symbolism of these two prints need
hardly occupy us here. It is sufficient to note that Hogarth is looking
with fresh eyes at the symbolic potential of the cat.

The cat is unashamedly a 'witch familiar' symbol in the engraving
which shows Hudibras routing the quack astrologer Sidrophel and his
companion Whacum, who have all the lower-level symbols of their art
of sortilege and necromancy about them. In this print, the cat has much
the same significance as the embryo preserved in the bottle, the skeleton,
the stuffed alligator and so on – it is part and parcel of the traditional
symbolism of demonism. One wonders if it is Hogarth's humour which
has him portray in the horoscope chart the planets Saturn and Mars in
opposition (or conflict), for Mars is the planet of aggression (the out-

raged Hudibras) and Sidrophel the 'pretending Wise Man' (the planet Saturn). The rest of the chart is sheer nonsense – it is not a horoscope at all – which would reflect further on Sidrophel's competence. Many literary interpreters have suggested that Samuel Butler's Sidrophel, who claimed to have discovered an elephant on the Moon, but had in fact a mouse in his telescope, represented Sir Paul Neal, a member of the newly formed Royal Society. Could this delightful historical footnote be reflected in the fact that the telescope is on one side of the floor, below Sidrophel? On the other side is the cat, at the foot of Hudibras: by this device Hudibras is symbolically associated with the cat, and may be regarded as hunting the 'mouse' Sidrophel.

Far more poignant, in the same *Hudibras* series, is the detail in 'Hudibras and the Skimmington', which as a composition is a parody of Carracci's 'Procession of Bacchus and Ariadne', but which depicts the rural custom for dealing with henpecked husbands and shrews. In this ritual the couple are tied together on a horse and escorted through their village to the mockery of their neighbours, amid bawdy and riot. Part of

Fig. 42   The ancient game of 'cat throwing' – a fifteenth-century misericord in the stall of St Sulpice, Diest (Belgium)

this riot involves the beating of a 'drum' (here a kettle) with a live cat, reminiscent of the cat-throwing games which were one of the entertainments of the mediaeval realm (figure 42). The old customs die out more slowly in the country villages, one might imagine, until one turns to the print of the Stages of Cruelty (figure 40).

Hogarth's symbolism is usually multi-layered, refreshingly new, journalistic in intent and concerned with satire, as a result of which he very rarely uses the religious symbolism which had been sanctified by centuries. However, in the popular print which shows strolling actresses dressing in a barn he makes an exception to this general rule by portraying in a footnote symbolism a cat playing with a crossed orb, the standard Christian symbol for the world. This is usually placed in the hands of God the Father, sometimes in the hand of Christ, as symbol of his domination over the entire world. In this detail Hogarth intended to show the kitten in playful domination over the world, and he reminds us that in the eighteenth century one of the slang words for prostitute was 'cat' – a use which has survived in the modern American term 'cathouse'. The actresses are not themselves prostitutes, but their state of undress would suggest the idea of prostitution, so that the word cat as a term of feminine weakness is still applicable. With regard to this symbolism, it is interesting that the play they are to rehearse is called *The Devil to Pay in Heaven* – the woman (or 'cat') has control of the Earth, while the other kitten is savaging the strings of the harp of Apollo which is supposed to symbolize the 'harmony' of the spheres, the eternal music. Between them, the kittens are destroying the earth and its ancient harmony. One other delightful piece of 'arcane' symbolism in this print is the monkey to the bottom far left, which is urinating into the helmet of Jupiter: in mediaeval symbolism the monkey (presumably because it chattered so much, like Air types) was adopted as a symbol of the element Air. It is an amusing conceit to have an Air symbol making Water into the helmet of a planetary god also associated with Air, for Water and Air were regarded as being inimical to each other in the universal flux of things. 'For wit and imagination', Horace Walpole rightly wrote of this print, it was 'the best of all his works'.

These notes do not exhaust the symbolism of Hogarth's cats. The feline appears in symbolic role in 'The Rake's Progress' and in 'Industry and Idleness', as well as in one or two other details of prints. However, sufficient has been said for us to realize the change which was taking place in the symbolic role of the cat in the eighteenth century as it was gradually cleared of the charge of being nothing more than a witch imp for all that Hogarth played with the traditional notion of the witch suckling her feline familiar (figure 43).

By the following century the cat could be used as a non-demonic symbol, or as a humorous thing, even in circumstances where a double meaning was intended. At Shrugborough there is an elaborate cat monument, one of several follies which are found in this landscape. It is said to commemorate the ship's cat which accompanied Admiral Anson on his many sea voyages. In some ways the Shrugborough monument is not really a folly, since it is an impressive enough memorial in the classical style – yet there is one genuine feline folly of a rather bizarre kind at Woolverstone near Ipswich, in what used to be a Gothic revival cottage formerly used for smuggling. The story tells how a cat was used as a secret signal between two smuggling fraternities: if the cat was sitting on the window ledge, it was safe to proceed with the movement of contra-

Fig. 43   Witch suckling a familiar cat. Detail of William Hogarth's engraving 'Credulity, Superstition and Fanaticism', 1762. The print is essentially a satire on Methodism, and on the credulous reaction to such 'psychic' phenomena of Hogarth's day as the 'Cock Lane Ghost', the Bilson Boy, Glanvil's 'Sadducismus Triumphatus', and so on. This credulity is not only that of the mob, and of the congregation, but also of the ministers of the church

band. The gothic window is a sham, painted into the recess, and in the second lancet from the left is painted the cat, a permanent symbol of the assessment that all is well with the smuggling world.

The eccentric naturalist and traveller Charles Waterton, who developed new methods of taxidermy, had a portrait done to illustrate one of his advanced and proficient books on his travels in which behind him is the head of a disconsolate-looking cat on a bust, resting upon a book. One might take this feline as a tongue-in-cheek commentary on the standard reference to antique busts which formed part of the ubiquitous paraphernalia in the portraits of more serious squires and gentlemen. However, the cheeky cat's head is probably a somewhat obvious reference to one of Waterton's more famous exploits. In the spirit of the eccentric travellers, he had brought back many strange animals from abroad – the majority of which had been improved by the art of taxidermy, at which he excelled. One of these imports was his so-called 'Nondescript', which caused a considerable stir in academic circles and in the popular imagination. In reality it was the stuffed head of a Red Howler monkey which Waterton had cleverly manipulated in the stuffing to suggest the appearance of a near-human creature of unknown species. Some claim that the sub-human portrait was intended to represent the appearance of an official in the Treasury who had vexed Waterton by imposing heavy duties on the animals which had been shipped back from his exotic travels. Perhaps the moggy head in Waterton's portrait is meant to be the cat among the pigeons?

The realm of cat-symbolism in modern art is so vast as to deserve a special treatment of its own, yet we cannot complete a survey of the symbolism of the everlasting cat without a passing reference to Henri Rousseau, the French painter. Rousseau was one of the world's greatly misunderstood artists, often dismissed as a 'Sunday Painter', yet in fact one of the most prolific and professional artists of the time, a friend of the leading painters and intellectuals of his day, from Toulouse Lautrec, Braque and Picasso to the poet Apollinaire. It is an affront to his greatness to consider his pictures as so many primitive decorations: indeed some of his paintings include among their subjects the most powerful cat images of modern art.

The intensity of the lion's eyes in 'The Dream' which Rousseau painted in 1910, with the extraordinary nude portrait of his wife Yadwigha, or the surrealistic lion beneath the full moon, sniffing at the sleeping woman of 'The Sleeping Gypsy', (1897) and the 'Tiger Devouring a

Gazelle' (1891) are each masterpieces, replete with arcane symbolism.

We may see something of the original force of Rousseau's secret symbolism if we examine the portrait he made of the French writer Pierre Loti (figure 44) in 1906, possibly to celebrate Loti's election to the Académie Française. Loti is wearing a strange fez-like hat, perhaps to

Fig. 44   Henri Rousseau. Portrait of Pierre Loti, 1910. Kunsthaus, Zurich. The graphic relationship between the cigarette-bearing fingers and the four chimneys (one of which is 'smoking') relate to one line of philosophy in this oil painting, while the relationship between the faces of cat and Loti point to another

remind one of the recent success of his book *Au Maroc*, which gives an account of his journey through Morocco to the capital, Fez. He is shown with a cat because Loti was well-known as a great cat-lover, and wrote repeatedly about his pets. This cat, with its curious lateral stripes, is an integral part of a well-organized symbolism. In order to reach into one of the levels of meaning within the picture we must cast aside the usual approach to art, and follow the graphic logic of the design which speaks a language of its own: note, for example, the way the four horizontal splashes of white on the legs of the cat 'echo' the four verticals of the chimneys behind the man. This emphasis on the four strong lines is echoed on the other side of the canvas in the man's hands, the fingers of which are at an angle, being neither vertical nor horizontal. It is significant that the man holds in these fingers a cigarette, so that the man himself, as well as one of the chimney stacks, is 'smoking'.

The full significance of this remarkable picture is not of concern to us here, as our chief interest lies in the cat. The man, like the chimney, is smoking – which is to say that he, as much as the factory behind him, is a part of the industrial world which weaves its poisons into the world. The curiously placed chimney and the clumsy hand are the two extremes of a compositional diagonal relating to 'civilized life'. The balance to this diagonal, which runs as a diagonal across the other half of the picture, is the cat and the tree which seems to grow from the man's shoulders in just the same way as the chimneys do. This diagonal represents the polarities of life – of unspoiled nature.

There is a progression in this symbolism, however, for the foliage of the trees merges with the man's head (that is, with his thinking), so that he has not lost all contact with pristine nature. The cat represents a stage nearer to 'civilization', for it is a domesticated cat, presumably one of Loti's pets. It is the man himself who symbolizes the ultimate stage of 'civilization', for he holds the cigarette, pushing into the foreground the pollution of the chimneys in the background.

This picture incorporates one of the most evocative and powerful of feline symbols, for it intimates that man has already gone too far into the realm of matter, into that realm where the world is no longer the object of love but has become subject to man's own poisons. In contrast, the cat appears to remain serenely aloof from this polluted realm, and it is from the cat (indeed, from the animal realm as a whole) that man should attempt to learn the lost secrets of nature. This cat, as a symbol of a saving natural grace, has come a long way since mediaeval times.

PART II

The Hellish Cat

Chapter Six

THE DEMONIC CAT

Whie witches are turned into cats Bodin
alledgeth no reason, and therefore . . . I saie,
that witches Are curst queanes, and manie times
scratch one another, or their neighbours by the
faces; and therefor perchance are turned into
cats. But I have put twentie of these
witchmongers to silence with this one question;
to wit, Whether a witch that can turne a woman
into a cat, etc: can also turne a cat into a
woman?

REGINALD SCOT

In her beautifully written *Extraordinary Cats* Olivia Manning sets out succinctly the history of the cat when she writes of the 'tough, unbiddable, little animal that, once worshipped as a god, later harassed as an agent of the devil, tortured as a symbol of wickedness and burnt as a consort of witches, has had to suffer more than its share of human stupidity'.

The spiritual origins of the cat may be experienced when one contemplates the magnificent Egyptian bronze in the British Museum, the so-called 'Gayer-Anderson Cat', named after its donor, Pasha 'John' Gayer-Anderson (figure 3). As Egyptian statuary goes, this is relatively late, probably having been cast in the Roman period, a few decades before the birth of Christ. The gold nose-ring and ear-rings are still intact, and on the cat's forehead is the sacred scarab, on its incised collar, the 'Udjat' or Eye of Horus, which marks it out as a holy cat. This was the truly spiritual archetypal cat, alert, mysterious and charged with feline grace. How was it possible that this lovely creature could spawn demons – how could such a divine animal fall from grace to become the familiar impish companion of witches?

The answer to this question may be had if we move further back into time – into the eighteenth dynasty, which corresponds to circa 1400 BC – to the Temple of Mut near modern Karnak, where hundreds of colossal cat statues were carved on the orders of Amenophis III. Very many of these black-granite figures are preserved in the Museum in Cairo and in the British Museum, and it is said that over 600 similar giant cats from the Mut Temple have been accounted for. The giant cats, with the ankh life-symbol in one paw and the solar disc behind their heads, are all images of the goddess Sekhmet, 'the cat-headed goddess who brought destruction on the enemies of the sun god Ra'.

It was this life-preserving cat-headed goddess who fell, and from whom the mediaeval church made demons. As Richard Mores says, 'the Christian Church sought to ignore the cat, in a natural reaction against those pagan religions which had worshipped it.' In this lie the seeds of the mediaeval growth which perceived the cat as at best the minion of the Devil, at worst the Devil himself. 'Only idiots', says the author of *The Devil's Bible*, 'refuse to acknowledge that all cats are in pact with the Devil.' In 1233 Gregory IX took the anti-cat league even further, for he said that the heretics (among whom were numbered the witches) worshipped the Devil in the form of a black tom cat. This notion is expressed time and time again in the arcane symbolism of European art, and Gregory was merely giving expression to an idea which was already widely accepted, for some of the sculpted images of the Devil from long before his day portray his Satanic Majesty with feline features. Among the most interesting cat-like faces are those found on the now incomplete twelfth-century symbolic sculpture at the top of the 'Staircase of the Dead' in the monastery of Sacra di San Michele, which towers over the Val di Susa in Italy (figure 45). Two of the demonic heads are on the pillars of the so-called 'zodiacal arch' (which is actually a constellation arch), while another is on a capital in front of this, almost certainly sculpted by the master Nicholas. This long-tongued demon with the cat's face (figure 45) is persuading Cain to commit the first murder: the Latin inscription on the abacus of the capital translates 'Righteous Abel dies, killed by the cudgel of his brother.' There is little doubt that the murder is instigated by this feline Satan.

The exquisite wooden carvings on the fifteenth-century choir stalls of
San Sulpice in Diest (Belgium), contain many very interesting esoteric
symbols such as the 'sea-knight', the harpy and monstrous demons.
Among these is the image of a man carrying a cat over his shoulder. The
man is laughing, and the over-sized cat looks distinctly uncomfortable.
The image has been interpreted by art-historians as relating to a popular
mediaeval activity in which living cats were thrown for 'sport', a cruel
game presumably justified by the notion that cats were intrinsically evil.

Another of the Diest misericords shows a man pushing a dog on a one-
wheeled cart. Under normal circumstances, the dog should be pulling
the man, and this is an example of one of the numerous mediaeval
allegories often called 'the World Upside Down'. The carving reminds
one of the observation made by the esotericist P. D. Ouspensky, in his
book *In Search of the Miraculous*, where he records that as a child he had a
book which contained humorous pictures in the world-upside-down

*Fig. 45 Demonic cat on the capital of one of the columns at the top of the 'Staircase of
the Dead', in Sagra di San Michele, Val di Susa, Italy. The carving is probably of the
early thirteenth century*

tradition, but that even as a boy he had observed such strange things in the world that the world-the-right-way-up seemed equally weird. Perhaps the image of the man throwing the cat among the Diest misericords belongs to this sequence of images, for according to mediaeval belief the reality was that the cat had the demonic power to throw the man – to throw him off balance spiritually.

The secret symbolism of the Egyptian priests entered into Europe in many disguises, but perhaps the most fantastic were in demonic form. The black-pact grimoires which proliferated in Europe after the fifteenth century and which described how demons might be conjured up contain lists of the most frightful of demons, some of which are merely the ancient pagan gods reduced to demonological status by Christian writers. The ram-headed Amun is scarcely disguised in the demon

Fig. 46   Feline-headed demon catching fish. Detail of the right wing of the triptych The Temptations of St Anthony, *by Hieronymus Bosch. Museu Nacional de Arte Antiga, Lisbon*

Amon, who has horns and the head of what might well be a goat. A few of this ghastly crew have feline ancestry, for they have the heads of cats, tigers or 'pards' (as leopards or panthers were called indiscriminately). Several of the imaginatively conceived demons in the work of Hierony-mus Bosch appear to have a feline ancestry. We have seen in chapter 5 one or two of the arcane meanings in his direct use of the cat as a symbol in other contexts, but it is worth glancing here at one good example of this painter's feline demons in the panels of 'The Temptations of Saint Anthony' in Lisbon (figure 46). As with most of Bosch's work, this paint-ing has been subjected to much critical appraisal, yet we appear to be no nearer understanding all the details of his arcane and secret symbolism, even though it may be admitted that he did work for an heretical sect for whom most of the symbols were fairly transparent in meaning. The feline demon in figure 46 is reaching from under a red tapestry and grasping at a dead fish, which still has the fatal arrow sticking from its side. He is snarling up at a naked woman, who appears to be entangled in a net grasped in the talons of a drinking demon, above the feline demon.

It is often misleading to interpret details from a picture without refer-ence to the overall significance of the picture as a whole, but in this case the demonic attack on the monk Saint Anthony (the overall theme) per-mits us to see these demonic details within a religious context. The fish is, of course, a fairly standard symbol for the Christ, and so the transfixed fish in the hands of a demon may be taken as a symbol of Christian des-pair ('the dead Christos'). The woman who is half hidden in the trunk of a tree is a richly evocative symbol, for at first glance we may take it that she represents Venus, since she appears to be making the classical 'Venus Pudens' gesture with her right hand. However, a closer survey shows that this is not her own hand, but the hand of a demon which, rather than making a modest gesture, is reaching for her private parts. Just as the Christian symbol of the fish is debased, and turned into its opposite (a dead Christ is inconceivable in Christian terms, of course), so the female Venus is being demoted, and is part of the sexual symbolism of the painting. The transparent veil which binds her is perhaps a veil of initiation, which is said to drop from the eyes of those who are permitted to legitimately look into the spiritual realm. Here again this symbolism is utterly debased, for the naked woman does not look upwards into the spiritual realm where Christ is King, but downwards into the demonic levels where the Christ is symbolically killed. The monstrous demon

Fig. 47   Haborym, a cat-headed demon of indendiarism, from Collin de Plancy's Dictionnaire Infernal, 1863

with the veil is being poured red wine, which it is clearly about to drink. Is this yet another slur on the wine of the Eucharist? Perhaps it is, since there is a red liquid pouring down the side of the dead tree trunk (symbol of the cross?), and running on the hand of the naked woman. Even within this small detail of the Bosch panel we see a bewildering number of arcane references showing how the Christian belief and ritual is mocked by the demons.

As we have seen, the origin for this bevy of cat-headed demons is the Egyptian goddess Bast, Bastet, or Bubastis. It was inevitable that such an unlikely combination of female body and cat-face (figure 11) in a pagan statue or fresco should induce the Christians to trace in it the lineaments of a demon. This is certainly the reason why so many of the mediaeval grimoires list demons who, when conjured into the magical circles, have the appearance of faces of cats.

The most fearsome of these demons was Haborym, sometimes called Aini, a triple-headed monster pictured by the popular occultist Collin de

Plancy as having the head of a viper, a humanoid face and a rather charming pussy-cat head emerging from his right collar bone (figure 47). In his right hand Haborym grasps a torch, a reminder that he is supposed to be the demon who concerns himself with incendiarism.

Flauros is no pussy cat, however, for the head is much more that of the leopard (Plate 7), which corresponds to the appearance which this demon is said to take when he first appears on the material plane when called before the conjurer from his magical circle. This feline Flauros is invoked by those who wish to get their own back against the demons for slights real or imaginary, for it seems that he is prepared to go against his own clan, as well as being famous among demonologists for destroying enemies by means of fire. He has a special reputation for being untruthful, however, which is perhaps unfortunate in one who is often conjured by magicians anxious to learn about the future.

There is something to be learned from these two demons, for both Haborym and Flauros, besides having cat heads, are also concerned with fire. It is in this dual aspect that we see distinct traces of the Egyptian mythology, for the cat-headed Bubastis was a 'cat and fire goddess'. Bubastis had several names, but one of them meant 'Little Cat', the Egyptian sound for which was 'Mew' or 'Mau'. According to some specialists this was the source of the word for the demon 'Mahu' in Shakespeare's *King Lear*, in the refrain sung by demented Edgar:

> The prince of darkness is a gentleman:
> Modo he's call'd, and Mahu.

One wonders what inspired the Bard to have the cats and witches leaping around the flames of a fire. However, more about this 'Mahu' and the witch-cat later.

The leopard-headed Flauros is a famous demon for he is listed among the 72 demons of the grimoire known as the *Lemegeton*, supposed to have been written by King Solomon, though, of course, the oldest manuscripts known do not date beyond the Middle Ages. Another three-headed demonic monster, Bael, is probably older, however, for this demon was originally the Semite god Baal, worshipped in Egypt even under Rameses II (1292–25 BC). It was this Baal who gave us the name of one of the most famous of all demons, 'Lord of the Flies', whose title is supposed to have been 'Baal-Zebub', meaning 'Lord of the Dunghill'. How Bael entered the oldest stream of demonic literature is uncertain, but he figures as one of the most horrific of the many demons listed in the late mediaeval Enochian literature, which insisted that the demons were originally angels who agreed to sacrifice their angelic state by uniting with women in sexual encounters, and thus falling deeply into the material condition. The earliest Enochian literature does not give descriptions of Bael but by the time occultists began to give accounts of the astral forms which they saw when they conjured demons, he has the head of a cat, sometimes that of a toad.

The nineteenth-century occultist Collin de Plancy depicts him with three heads (Plate 20). The connexion with fire is not as obvious as with Flauros and Haborym, but it could be that the notion of the 'inner fire' is continued in the fact that the demon is conjured because he is able to satisfy all cravings or 'inner burnings and desires'. De Plancy is merely following the occult tradition when he depicts Bael as having a central human head with to the left the long-lipped head of a frog or toad, and to the right that of a cat; yet his notion that the body is that of a spider is a personal idea.

The seasoned occultist will trace almost all the three-headed demons to the three-headed, or three-person gods of the pagan pantheons. In the Indian pantheon the triad was Brahma-Vishnu-Siva, but in the origins of the European imagery the triad was entirely lunar, as Diana-Hecate-Luna, the 'Diva triformis' or the 'Tergemina'. Even so, the Christians developed their own cat mythology which had undertones of an occult lore which would surprise the majority of people.

There is a mediaeval legend that the Devil had tried to emulate God by creating Man. The Devil did not have the same power as God, and the end product of his endeavour was a skinless cat – a most piteous looking creature. When St Peter saw the cat, he made for it a fur coat, and it is for this reason that the fur is said to have such magical properties. As we have seen, the black fur of a tom cat is said to brush away a stye, while the tail of a tortoiseshell may be used to stroke away warts. Another superstition insists that if the entire tail is buried beneath the threshold of a house, the family who dwells within will have good health.

The symbolism behind this curious legend seems to support the mediaeval notion that the cat was an evil creature – after all, it was made accidentally by the Devil. Yet when we look at the story closely we see that while the cat may have been the result of an accident, it was perfected by St Peter, by one of the Christian apostles. Could the story be an allegory of man, who is made partly by the Devil and yet will find completion by the Christian message?

One wonders indeed if St Peter was chosen to figure in this legend because of his connexion with the sea? He was after all one of the fishermen chosen by Christ, and the link between the cat and the sea is confirmed in many legends and superstitions. In her book on animal folklore, Venetia Newell records that certain Scarborough sailors' wives would keep a black cat at home to ensure the safety of their husbands at sea. We shall have an opportunity to examine the sea legend of the cat a little more closely when we look into witchcraft and the cat familiar (chapter 7), but it is worth recording that among the rustic drugs and charms recorded by Percy Jeffrey in his *Whitby Lore and Legend* is one to cure 'pelsey' or the falling sickness of palsy, which involved taking the blood of a white dove and 'ye head of a black cat'. In another part of his interesting narrative he points out that accounts of good or bad fortune attached to a black cat are contradictory. A stray black cat taking up a dwelling in a house would be regarded as lucky for the place, but its presence on board ship would not be tolerated. However, he notes that the sailors on the ill-fated ship *Rohilla* which sank off Whitby towards the end of the last century, had a black cat mascot which was saved from the wreck. From a diary entry for 31 May 1797 he records:

> Saw three black cats last night so did not go to market to-day fearing somne evil, but it turned out well as Betty was taken with spasms and might have died had I not stayed at home and she is the best milker of all I have, this omen for ill brought nought but good.

Even in the early fifteenth century, before the full force of the witch-craft delusions and 'heresies' had been unleashed on Europe, we find many occultists and demonologists insisting that the cat is linked with witchcraft. The Italian occultist Antonio Guaineri wrote in his *De egritudinibus capitis* of the incubus, the lewd demon which was supposed to approach sleeping women and have intercourse with them. He personally appears to think that the phenomenon of the incubus is little more than a physical sensation caused by 'vapours' arising from the body, resulting in a sense of oppression, but he is careful to point out that others maintain that the incubus is the result of witchcraft: 'our common people call them "strigae" or "zobianae", and say that they often assume the shape of cats.' The idea was not very widespread, however, for it was generally believed that the demonic incubus preferred to adopt the shape of a full-grown man or a satyr (though when seeking the favours of sleeping witches, he was supposed to take the form of a goat).

In later times, when the theory of the incubus was developed in some detail, it was often claimed that the demon had to take a dead body as the instrument of his pleasure.

The cat suffers greatly under the pen of the French lawyer and expert in witchcraft trials Henri Boguet. He personally supervised the torture of the unfortunate suspect Françoise Secretain, charged with bewitching an eight-year-old girl who, as a result, had become possessed with devils, including one which was called Cat. Boguet later recorded:

> Her father and mother were anxious for their daughter's health and did not cease praying all night. The next morning at dawn the girl was worse than usual and kept foaming at the mouth; at last she was thrown to the ground and the devils came out of her mouth in the shape of balls as big as the fist and red as fire, except the Cat, which was black.

Françoise Secretain was burnt alive, and much of Boguet's *Discours des Sorciers* is based on reflections on her case and related trials.

Boguet also wrote of the sexually orientated incubus:

> The ugliness and deformity lies in the fact that Satan couples with witches sometimes in the form of a black man, sometimes in that of some animal, as a dog or a cat or a ram . . . Françoise Secretain confessed that her demon appeared sometimes as a dog sometimes as a cat . . . when he wished to have carnal intercourse with her.

The instance that the incubus was cat-like is not supported by many of the illustrations of the fulsome demon. For example, there is a fourteenth-century illustration in the Bibliothèque Nationale in Paris which shows a succubus in bed with the mother of Merlin. It was widely believed in the late mediaeval period that Merlin was born of an incubus, yet this demon taking his pleasure beneath the sheets is not at all cat-like, and really nothing more than the standard form of horned demon.

The odd thing is that for all the cat had an evil reputation in the late mediaeval period there are records which show that the liver of a black cat was sometimes used in the act of exorcism, as part of the ritual for driving demons out of those possessed. This is almost the opposite of what we might expect of such an 'evil' animal, unless, of course, there was that elusive sympathetic magic involved, and the invading devils were being driven out on the principle of like attracting like, one evil attracting another. Symphorien Champier, who wrote in the early six-teenth century, held the well-entrenched opinion that witches did exist, though he believed that the sabbat was illusory and the deeds to which the witches and warlocks confessed were more involved with falsehood than with truth. He had no doubt that diabolic sorcery existed, yet expressed the opinion that it could be countered only by the aid of 'good angels' (by what we might nowadays call 'White Magic') or by the offi-cial exorcisms of the Church – not by means of such substances as the liver of a black cat.

August Digot records some of the superstitions of approximately the same period in the district of Lorraine. It seems that before the villagers danced in front of their bonfires lit to celebrate St John's Eve, they would suspend one or two cats above the flames, presumably to rid the area of evil, prior to driving their domestic animals through the smoke to pre-serve them from disease. In some parts of France and Italy it was usual for the St John's Day burning of cats on bonfires to be merely a cruel preparation of talismans and charms: after the ritual burning, the ashes of the burned cats were carefully scraped up and preserved as potent magic.

The custom of burning cats as symbolic of demonic power was not limited to the Continent, for during the anti-Papist riots in Elizabethan England cats were sometimes adopted as symbols of the 'diabolical Pope'. It is recorded that during the coronation of Queen Elizabeth I, a huge wickerwork effigy was made of the Pope, into which were pushed a number of stray cats. After parading this monstrous image through the streets of London, the perpetrators threw it into a huge bonfire, pretend-ing that the screams of the cats were the noises of the demons in the dying Pope. Since it was widely believed that black cats attended witches' sabbats, it was customary for the villagers to cut off their tails, in the assumption that this would prevent them from going with their witch-mistresses.

At a later point we shall examine some of the possible reasons why the cat should deserve this reputation for evil, but it is worth observing that the explanations given in the 'scientific' texts of the later mediaeval period are charged with illogicality and superstition. The Swiss occultist Thomas Erastus, writing his *De occultis pharmacorum potestatibus* in 1574, distinguished two different species of occult virtue, and in describing one of these he instances several examples of antipathy between ani-mals – the fleeing of a sheep from a wolf, when it has seen it for the first time only; how the grunting of a pig will frighten an elephant or the crowing of a cock terrify the otherwise brave lion. It is, he maintains, for the same reasons of 'occult virtue' that some men dislike cheeses and others cannot stand cats. All these notions have been derived from much older sources, and we may presume that they had never been tested, yet we are still left with the question why the cat had such an undeserved reputation.

The remarkable sixteenth-century artist Hans Baldung Grien left behind a large number of drawings and prints showing groups of witches in lascivious poses, transvecting or occupying themselves with spells and flying ointments (Plate 21). It is highly significant that all the most important of these pictures show a cat in the foreground, as the standard symbolism for witchcraft. This use of a cat in a witchcraft image may be derived from the notion that witches and warlocks worshipped the Devil in the form of a black tom or may be intended to point to a much older stream of symbolism. Aristotle had said that the female cat was highly lecherous, and for this reason the cat was sometimes used as symbol of sexual proclivity. One gets the feeling from the Baldung Grien drawings and prints that it is the sexual element, rather than the black magic, which intrigues him: his women and crones are usually naked, and making exuberant or sensual physical gestures. We are reminded that in mediaeval times the word 'cat' was slang for a prostitute.

The Louvre and Vienna drawings of 1514 were each copied with varying degrees of success by other artists in his circle, and in each case the cat plays an important part in the salacious company. This is also true of the magnificent two-colour woodcut of 1510 (Plate 21), which shows the same theme taken up by Dürer (figure 48) of a witch transvecting backwards on a goat, along with the more Baldung-like theme of naked crones making evil brews in a desolate landscape. The familiar cat to the right of this picture sensibly has its back to the proceedings. There is a contour copy of a witchcraft scene by Baldung in Colburg which shows a shapely naked woman being approached by a witch, with the same impish feline on the couch upon which the woman reclines, but this is a somewhat sedate pussycat in comparison with the fearsome creature in the pen drawing of 1515, now in Besançon library.

A very interesting 'adaptation' of one of Baldung's drawings shows a cat in the foreground of a bevy of hideous naked witches, who are rubbing the magical flying ointment on their bodies in preparation for transvecting to the sabbat. The cat is reading a book. The general view of this delightful vignette of symbolism is that the cat is the Devil himself reading a grimoire. However, there is a deeper symbolism in the vignette which appears to have evaded the attention of art historians. The book is actually upside down: this we may tell from the fact that the only symbol on the page which may be distinguished is itself upside down. This symbol is a most interesting one for it is the sigil of the demon Och, one of the seven major demons, and is linked with the Sun itself. Och is indeed the

Fig. 48   Witch Riding Backwards on a Goat, *etching* (circa *1502) by Albrecht Durer*

demonic spirit of the Sun, and figures in many of the diabolical grimoires. The witches' cat, associated for millennia with the Moon, is contemplating the inverted symbol of the Sun-demon: it is a piece of symbolism which would not have been missed by the contemporaries of Grien, but is easily overlooked today. In non-demonic pictures it was quite usual to put the symbols for the Sun and the Moon in the upper part of the picture (for example, over the head of the crucified Christ), but in a drawing dedicated to evil it is a clever piece of arcane design to have these two symbols at the very bottom of the picture, clothed in demonic forms.

Not long after Grien was making these illustrations the French witchcraft specialist and judge Bodin wrote his awful *Demonomanie*, which was published in 1580. Most of the material he used in his puerile and vindictive arguments against witches was very old, but he had the habit of writing as though he had personally witnessed and tested the matters under question. He had no doubt at all that witches could fly

Fig. 49 *Drawing of the witch, demonic goat, and cat, after the sculpture on the west front of Lyons Cathedral. The original is probably thirteenth-century, and similar symbols are found in several French churches and cathedrals*

through the air, that there were such demons as the incubus and succubus, and that witches would make real poisons. Among the witchcraft poisons are those made from the brain of a cat or the head of a raven.

The sculptured stone panel in Lyons Cathedral has been interpreted as a picture of a witch riding a man she had turned into a goat, and the creature being whirled around the goat's head as a cat. The whole group is said to be on its way to the sabbat. There is little evidence for this interpretation, however. Though we may be reasonably sure that the naked woman does represent a witch, and the man-goat she rides is probably the Devil – one doubts, however, that the animal aloft is a cat (figure 49). If the sculpture is of the fourteenth century, as some suggest, it is unlikely that the group is heading for the sabbat, as the notion itself had not been developed even in witchcraft literature.

In the mediaeval period the cat had figured in magical recipes of a darker kind. The great astrologer and magician Cecco d'Ascoli, who was burned at the stake at Florence in 1327, named the four great demonic rulers of the four directions Oriens, Amaymon, Paymon and Egim, and said that these beings were of such high and noble nature that prior to conjuration human flesh or blood must be sacrificed to them. If neither of these was available, the only animal worthy of such sacrifice was the cat.

Of course, the view of the cat as a demonic being is not restricted to Europe, for stories of gigantic cat-demons are found in legends and myths throughout the world (figure 50). In a legend told by Hadland Davis in *Myths and Legends of Japan* we learn how the eldest maiden daughter of a family was required to be offered as sacrifice to evil mountain spirits who adopted the form of felines and were headed by a monstrous cat. On the day before the anticipated sacrifice, a samurai was resting in a mountain temple when he was awakened by a party of spirit cats dancing around and shouting, 'Tell it not to Shippeitaro.' On the following day the same samurai arrived at the village where the sacrifice had to be made. Assuming that the monsters were linked with the cat-spirits which he had seen on the previous night, he asked who Shippeitaro might be. It turned out that this was the fierce and brave dog which belonged to the headman of the village. The samurai fetched the dog, and helped carry the woman into the mountains. Instead of returning with the other men, he and the dog hid behind the cage in which the woman had been imprisoned. When the spirit cats appeared they were accompanied by a most ferocious tom cat, who pulled open the cage

Fig. 50   Detail of a nineteenth-century Japanese woodcut by Kuniyoshi, showing the transformation of the Okabe witch into a cat

door to grasp his human meal. Shippeitaro leapt out and grabbed the monster in his teeth, while the samurai drove off the minion cats with his sword. After this débâcle, the monster spirits left the mountains altogether and no sacrifices were demanded again.

Among the Quechua Indians of South America there is a most powerful evil cat-spirit named Ccoa, whose small size (it is said to be about 2 feet long, with a 1-foot tail) belies its awesome nature. The eyes of Ccoa are said to be phosphorescent, and from its pupils, as from its ears, there streams a permanent hail. The Quechua witch-doctors are said to derive their power from him, though he in turn is said to work for an even greater evil being.

Ccoa reminds us of the legendary cat of the Old Irish tales, the so-called 'King of the Cats', who bore the name Iruscan. One of the legends of Iruscan, in his dealings with the poet Senchan, is recounted on pages 53–4.

Perhaps there is some connexion between this Irish cat and the demon-cats which figure in the Taigheirm or Taghairm rituals associated with the Scottish Hebrides. The historian Bede tells us how until the eighth century the island of Lewis was not only destitute of men, fruit, trees and plants, but was the renowned meeting place of evil spirits, until they were exorcized by the monk Cudbrecht. However, one doubts that the exorcism was complete, for there are several witchcraft stories attached to the island (especially to the stone circles of Callanish), and records of the eighteenth century indicate that diabolical cat sacrifices were practised on the island.

The name Taigheirm for the cruel sacrificial rituals is interesting for it appears to be linked with the Gaelic word *taibhse* which means a 'spectre', 'vision' or, by extension, 'starveling animal'. The derived Gaelic *taibhsearachd* means approximately 'second sight', while a *taibhsear* is a seer. The second part of the word is derived from *gairm*, meaning 'a call'.

This connexion between the ritual and the notion of second sight is expressed in one reason given for the practice of cat sacrifice in the Western Isles, for after the Taigheirm the magicians were able to demand of the demons they had conjured by means of the cat sacrifices the gift of second sight. The terrible ritual lasted for a period of four days and nights, commencing at midnight on the Friday, the day of Freya. The cats chosen for the purpose were dedicated to the Devil, and then one by one roasted alive on spits in front of a huge fire. It is said that when the sacrifice had been continued for a certain period of time, infernal spirits would manifest in the form of cats and add to the racket of the felines being tortured. At length, a gigantic demon king of cats would appear. It is believed that these cruel rituals were practised in the Western Isles until the middle of the sixteenth century, the last one being on Mull, when Allan MacLean received the gift of second sight.

Chapter Seven

THE CONSORT OF WITCHES

Robert George Tinbull of Marske, was spelled [be-
witched] on ye bridge ower an hour by Hester Dale, the
old witch of Marrick. His horse would not move until
Tom Wilsom came along with a wicken staff [a rowan
staff, a well-known specific against witchcraft]. Then
they both saw Aister [the witch] run ower the road as a
black cat. They both ken'd it was her, for she hath meant
him harm for a good spell. But the bridge is haunted.

from the diary of a Whitby man, dated 9 September 1757

We have seen how the debased cat of the later demonologies was once
upon a time the Egyptian goddess Sekhmet or Bastet whose part-feline
form was in turn echoed in the later demonic images of Flauros and
Haborym, and it is this fact which accounts for much of the imagery of
witchcraft which seems otherwise inexplicable and strange. However,
not all historians trace the 'Fallen Cat' back to the Egyptian pantheon,
for they maintain that there is sufficient feline imagery in the Roman
and Greek mythology to account for the later associations of the cat with
witchcraft and diabolism.

In Roman times the goddess of Liberty was represented as holding a
cup in one hand, a broken sceptre in the other, and with a cat lying at her
feet. This symbolism is often interpreted in the light of the cat's
renowned love for liberty, but it might just as easily be interpreted as one
of the symbols of the lower nature, prone at the feet of Liberty, in much
the same way as later statuary and pictures show the demons prone at

the feet of Christ and the saints. It was inevitable that when the ancient goddesses were debased and turned into demons, their attendant images should follow suit. What had been a sacred cat, companion to Isis the Queen of the Night, became a monstrous familiar, companion to the Queen of Darkness. Some explain the connexion between the cat and witches as derived from the classical story of Galanthis, the servant who helped Alcmene to give birth to Hercules, who was turned into a cat by the angry Fates and became a priestess of the lunar goddess Hecate. However, not all the stories of Galanthis have her changed to feline shape. According to Ovid she was turned into a lizard, but an equally popular version has her transformed into a weasel – and we have already noted the connexion in Roman times between the weasel and the cat.

The witches' familiar has a curious history, and has long thrown unfair aspersions on the company of cats. According to the witchcraft literature, the true familiar was a demon in disguise, and was a gift made by the Devil to each witch who was induced to attend a sabbat and join the diabolic band. Such familiars were sometimes called 'imps', and while some remained invisible save to their owners, others would appear in disguise in order to hide their true nature. If the sorry and sordid literature of the witchcraft trials is anything to go by, the most popular disguises adopted by these demonic gifts were as cats or frogs. As a result the witch is shown riding her broomstick or demon accompanied more often than not by her flying familiar cat. Whether such pictures are salacious or humorous, the imp is scarcely optional in images ranging from the bitter ironies of Goya (figure 2) to the children's imagery of Arthur Rackham.

As we have seen, by mediaeval times, the ancient love for the cat had been transformed by Christian superstition into hatred, and the cat was seen as an instrument of the Devil's whim: as Friedmann observes, in his detailed study of the imagery of Antonello da Messina, 'The cat was also an old, but relatively seldom used symbol of Heresy, because its ability to see in the dark likened it to those in touch with the evil spirits of darkness.' It goes without saying that supposed witchcraft was itself the prevalent heresy in the fifteenth and sixteenth centuries.

However, it might be more fair to look at the love of cats in our search for the connexion between witchcraft and the cat familiar. Since the superstition was that the familiar was a demon in disguise, the household pet of anyone suspected of witchcraft would immediately be taken

Fig. 51   The familiar cat of the Belvoir Witches. The three members of the Flower family, Joan and her two daughters Margaret and Phillipa (all from Bottesford, and working at Belvoir Castle), were accused of bewitching the children of the 6th Earl of Rutland. The crude cut, which shows a cat which figured in the trials, is from a pamphlet recording the story of the hanging of the daughters at Lincoln in 1617. Joan died under suspicious circumstances before coming to trial

for a demon, and as the most popular pet, the cat would be most frequently exposed to this suspicion. As a result few cases of witchcraft on record in the English documents do not mention the use of cats or kittens as familiars. In the sixteenth century George Giffard left an account of the magical nature of the familiars when he wrote, 'witches have their spirits, some hath one, some hath more, as two, three, four, or five, some in one likeness and some in another, as like cats, weasels, toads or mice, whom they nourish with milke or a chicken, or by letting them suck now and then a drop of blood.' In the awful literature of the witchcraft trials there are literally hundreds of similar examples of women condemned as witches mainly on the grounds that they had evil reputations, and kept household cats or dogs (figures 51 and 52).

Accounts of how the witches would suckle their familiars are on the edge of vampirism. Almost all the ancient grimoires, which give details of how one might raise demons, take it for granted that spirits of the evil kind will derive energy from blood, whether from animal sacrifice or from the veins of the magician. An example of feline vampirism (in which the case histories of witchcraft abound) is found in Samuel Petto's book, *A Faithful Narrative* (1652), where he describes how the witch Abre Grinset of Dunwich in Suffolk confessed that the Devil appeared to her as an attractive young man at first, but later in the form of 'a blackish Gray Cat or Kitling, that it sucketh' of a teat which was found by the searchers on her body. In the Edward Fairfax case at York (discussed on pages 180–1), a young child who was supposedly bewitched noticed that one of the witches suckled a white cat familiar called Fillie, which appears in the drawing attributed to Miles Gale in figures 53 and 54, and when later she saw another demonic spirit at the woman's breast, she said:

> Thou are a cunning witch, indeed to let thy spirit suck there upon thy pap's head, for nobody can find a mark upon thee.

This implies that the witch was supposed to feed her familiar from some irregular mark upon her body, the so-called witch-teat from which the

Fig. 52 A cat familiar, from 'A Rehearesall both straung and true, of hainous and horrible actes committed by . . . notorious Witches, apprehended at Winsore in the Countie of Barks . . . and exucuted on the 26 daye of Februarie laste Anno. 1579'. Familiar cats played an important role in the story of the Windsor witchcraft story

imp could suck blood rather than milk. The presence of such a teat, however small, or however much merely a wart or a pimple, was regarded as sufficient evidence for hanging a woman during the heyday of the witchcraft craze.

Perhaps also the old wives' tale which maintains that a cat should not be allowed near a sleeping child has its origins in a similar witchcraft belief. The rationale is that the cat might smother the child by nestling against its face, but some nurses insist that the cat would suck the baby's breath, and so deplete its life-forces.

The most famous English witchcraft trial case involving a named cat was known as 'the Chelmsford Witches', though the ladies concerned came from the Essex village of Hatfield Peverell. The trial is typical of the importance placed upon imps in regard to 'evidence', and seems in some respects to come down to the antics of a spotted cat with the unfortunate name of 'Sathan'. Most of the material relating to the trials at Chelmsford is taken from a sensational chapbook, plus a few of the

Fig. 53 Witch suspect, with her white cat-spirit called 'Fillie'. The drawing was allegedly done by the Reverend Miles Gale, the incumbent at Keighley, to illustrate the 'Daemonologia' manuscript of circa 1621, written by Edward Fairfax as his personal account of the Fewstone witchcraft trials, in which he claimed that his children had been bewitched by local women aided by talking cats, and other demonic familiars. The illustrated manuscript is now in the British Library

Fig. 54 *The witch suspect Jennet Deb, with her familiar cat-spirit 'Gibb', after the drawing allegedly done by the Reverend Miles Gale,* circa 1705. *British Library. According to the trial records, Gibb had the ability to speak. Oddly enough, the Fewstone witches, charged with bewitching the children of Edward Fairfax, were cleared of all charges*

trial records, which indicate that this impish Sathan was able to turn himself into a toad, as well as into a black dog. He was a cat of considerable antiquity, for the supposed witch Elizabeth Francis had been given him by her grandmother when she was twelve 'in the likeness of a white spotted cat', and was taught his name and (horror of horrors) how to feed him on bread and milk. She kept the cat for some sixteen years, and then, for reasons which are not clear, gave him to a Mother Waterhouse, 'telling her that she must call him Sathan'.

In the court indictments, it seems that bread and milk were not sufficient, for Elizabeth was also wont to feed the cat with her own blood. Although he was said to be a demon in disguise, he didn't appear to do Elizabeth much good. The allegations claimed that the cat could speak, and made her gifts which 'did wear away'. For each of these dubious gifts, Elizabeth was required to donate in return a drop of her own blood as food – the place she pricked to give such blood remaining as a mark upon her body. By means of this impish cat, she bewitched to death one Andrew and obtained an abortion for herself, as well as finding a husband by whom she had a child – 'Wherefor she willed Sathan her cat to kill the child, being about the age of half a year old, and he did so.' A survey of these long cases would suggest that the women were convicted by their own confessions, which might be obtained through all sorts of (illegal) tortures. For example, Mother Waterhouse 'confessed that falling out with one widow Gooday she willed Sathan to drown her cow . . . and falling out with another of her neighbours, he killed her three geese in the same manner . . .' The charges of 'evil doing' were proved and she was hanged on 29 July 1566 – as R. Hope Robbins says, 'possibly the first woman hanged for witchcraft in modern England'.

A later set of witchcraft trials in 'Chelmisforde', resulting in the execution of three women in April 1579, emphasizes the familiar-imp theme with its diabolic image of a cat familiar named Satan (Plate 22) on the title cover. It is most interesting that the blurb on this tract should spell the name for Satan in the same way as that of the unfortunate cat of the earlier trials: 'Set forthe to discover the Ambuthementes of Sathan, whereby he would surprise us lulled in securitie, and hardened with contempte of Gods vengeance threatened for our offences.'

In the case of witchcraft recorded during the sixteenth century, the woman called Gammer Alice Samuel was hanged on 7 April 1593 because the eldest daughter of Sir Robert Throckmorton had claimed that she was a witch, and had tried to suffocate her with frogs, toads and cats, the recognized 'familiars' of witchcraft lore. The three women (mother and two daughters) who died as a result of the celebrated case of witchcraft at Belvoir Castle, Leicestershire in 1617 suffered mainly because they owned a cat (figure 51). 'The principal charge against them,' wrote one historian, 'was their having a cat called Rutterkin; the supposed diabolical agent of their machinations.' The case of 'sorcerye', in which the sons of the sixth Earl of Rutland were supposed to have been bewitched to death, is recorded in the effigied witchcraft tomb in nearby Bottesford parish church. A similar case is recorded by Roger North, the brother of the Lord Chief Justice, who relates that in an Exeter trial an old woman was condemned to be hanged because a neighbour testified that she had seen a cat jump into the window of her cottage one evening, and had believed it to be the Devil. A cat and dog, clearly of demonic origin, figure in the curious story of Anne Bodenham told by Nathaniel Crouch in his *Kingdom of Darkness* 1688 (Plate 23).

A short time before the Samuel hanging, George Gifford of Maldon, Essex, had written his influential *Discourse of the Subtle Practise of Devils by Witches and Sorcerers* (1587). He tells of a witch who had a familiar in the form of a black cat which destroyed the animals of a farmer she disliked. The farmer appears to have countered this with his own black magic, however, for he is reported to have burnt one of his pigs alive, with the result that the witch's cat would no longer go near his farm. Gifford tells the stories in order to question the witchcraft delusion, his thesis being that an all-powerful Devil had no need of such minions as witches to do his evil. The familiars, such as the black cat, he regarded as delusions of the witches themselves:

> A witch cannot by a familiar, or by any craft, or any way hurt or weaken the life, health, or estate of any man by witchery with diseases or infirmity ... Because the hogs and the cow died are you sure the cat did hurt them? Might they not die of some natural causes, as you see both men and beasts are well, and die suddenly?

In the records of the Scottish witch trials there are many references to the belief that the cat was a witch-imp, a witch in disguise and even the witch or the Devil himself. It is recorded, for example, that in 1607 Isobel Grierson was burned for witchcraft mainly because of feline associations. Isobel had lived in Saltpans (the modern Prestonpans), and her neighbours had complained that she would walk around the village at night time, disguised as a cat and making an awful mewling sound. At her trial it emerged that she had cast a spell on one of her neighbours, and would appear at his fireside each night, sometimes in the form of a cat, sometimes in the form of a child: the neighbour eventually died, and Isobel was charged with his murder by witchcraft.

Scottish witchcraft literature is well endowed with demonic cats. Witches in Lanark (Strathclyde) were charged with riding to their sabbat on a cat, while those in Humbie (Lothian) were said to have baptized a cat as part of their diabolic practice. In 1596 the witches of Aberdeen were accused of changing their forms into the likeness of cats – the indictments reading that one suspect, Bessie Thom:

> accompanied with ... devilish companions and factions, transformed in other likeness, some in hares, some in cats, and some in other similitudes ... all danced about the Fish Cross.

Among the many extraordinary things to which the suspect witch Isobel Gowdie confessed (though again under extreme torture) was that on Lammas Day in 1659 her own coven disguised themselves in the form of cats, crows and hares, and went charging through the countryside, destroying the goods of their neighbours. However, we gather from the details of the magical recipe which Gowdie recorded as a means of achieving such a change of shape that instead of transforming themselves into cats, they merely developed the power to enter into the bodies of ordinary cats. The practices were quite different, for it was believed that shape-changing required a far more advanced knowledge of magic than merely 'demonic possession'.

During the trial of the infamous Greenock witch Marie Lamont, she confessed in 1662 that she and her coven assembled in Argowan where they met the Devil 'in the likeness of a black man, with cloven feett', who while talking to them raised his hands above his head and turned them all into cats. Her firnes (friends), Kettie Scot and Margaret Holm, both then in the 'likeness of kats', entered the house of Allan Orr, and partly ate a fish stolen from a barrel. This transformation was one thing, but the fact that they left the fish for Orr's wife to finish was quite another, since when she had eaten it, the unfortunate woman died. One of the stories of witchcraft 'repercussion' has survived in the account of the effigy of Lady Ann in St Michael's Church, Edmondthorpe (Plate 24) – perhaps a tale invented posthumously to account for the break in the marble wrist of the effigy.

The 'Thurso witches' cat-story gets very close to the traditional tales of repercussion. It began when a merchant called Montgomerie petitioned the local sheriff to rid his own house in Scrabster of an infestation of cats which, he reported, 'spoke among themselves'. Curiously enough, witchcraft was not suspected at this point, for the sheriff delayed in dealing with the nuisance, to a point where Montgomerie armed himself with sharp instruments and killed two of the cats, striking off the leg of a third. Shortly afterwards a suspect called Helen Andrew died suddenly, and at the same time another was drowned. A third old woman, Margaret Nin-Gilbert, was seen to have a leg missing. There are a number of variant tales as to how this was discovered, but the putrefied limb was used in evidence against her, and a few days later she confessed to the practice of witchcraft. Unfortunately, she died in prison after a few days – whether from excess of torture or from gangrene is not recorded.

During the extraordinary trials of the North Berwick witches in the late sixteenth century, one of those accused of attempting to murder King James admitted (albeit under extreme torture):

> that at the time when his majestie was in Denmarke, shee ... took a cat and christened it, and afterwards bounde to each part of that cat the chiefest parte of a dead man and severall joyntes of his bodie; and that in the night following, the saide cat was convayed into the middest of the sea by all these witches, sayling in their riddles or cives [sieves] ... and so left the saide cat right before the towne of Leith in Scotland; this doone, there did arise such a tempest in the sea, as a greater hasthe not bene seene, which tempest was the cause of the perishing of a boat or vessel comming over the town of Brunt Island ...

The suspect, Agnes Sampson, was later executed as a witch, after a trial largely directed by the king himself.

We have already seen some of the many taboos and superstitions connected with ship's cats. It was widely believed also that if a cat on board a ship licked its fur in the wrong direction, or scratched table legs with its claws, this would start a furious storm. Most significant among a whole battery of taboos was that if a ship's cat were thrown overboard, this would have the effect of raising a tempest. It is probably on this single taboo that the story of the witches of North Berwick drowning a cat was based.

The view of the cat as a 'witch familiar' was not confined to Britain. Indeed, there are probably more records of cat-witches and feline transformations in Germanic witchcraft literature. One notorious example occurred in Bergtheim in 1586, when a woman named Anna Winkelzipfel was burned as a witch because (it was claimed) she had disguised herself in the skins of black cats.

In Spain no artist used the cat with more symbolic effect in witchcraft imagery than Goya, especially in his famous 'Caprichos' series. In one etching the cat stands screeching on the back of a snake, which is grasped by a naked witch, herself being carried by a winged demon (figure 55). 'There goes the witch,' wrote Goya on the preparatory drawing, 'riding on the little crippled devil.' It is a witch instructress giving a first flying lesson to her pupil, and even this first aerial flight evokes the familiar cat. There is also a familiar witch-cat in '¿Donde va Mama?' (Where is Mother going?) (figure 56). This might be a nightmare, but Goya explains that it is a 'Mighty witch who because she has dropsy is

Fig. 55   Etching-aquatint by Goya, from his 'Caprichos'. Alla va Eso (There it goes): *Goya's commentary begins, 'There goes a witch, riding on the little crippled devil.' The etching apparently illustrates a witch instructress giving a first flying lesson to a pupil, with the indispensable cat familiar riding behind, curiously enough attached to the back of a snake held in the right hand of the witch*

taken for an outing by the best flyers.' Such a subject cannot fail to have its familiar cat, but why does Goya depict it hanging as though in grim death to the umbrella, like a parachutist out of time and place? We are in a more familiar setting with the two cats in the foreground of 'Ensayos' (Trials), which Goya tells us in a note is intended to show the trial of newly inducted witches on their first flight (figure 2). The witches are naked, both levitating in front of a horned monster. Two familiar cats, a skull and an earthenware jug are their paraphernalia. What is in the jug? Could it be blood? Just behind the cats we see half a trussed animal (it could be a dog, or even a cat). Has this been slaughtered prior to the diabolic incantations of levitation or transvection, as the dark grimoires insist? When the Flemish artist Bosch painted diabolical cats, he transformed their features so that they are seen to be half-demon, half-feline (Plate 17), but Goya makes his cats diabolical by a sort of chilling subtlety – their demonic state seen in the terror of their eyes rather than in any twisting of form. So it is with the naked women who consort with the demons through the ribald horror of the Spanish Caprichos.

One awful example of the cat-imp belief is the account of a trial of 300 children at Mohra in Sweden at the end of the seventeenth century. It was claimed that each of these children had been given a kitten by the Devil, and its diabolical duty was to steal butter, cheeses and other victuals for its master. Many of the children were found guilty, fifteen of them being executed, and 36 severely whipped for 52 successive Sundays at the doors of the local church.

On the whole the notion of the cat familiar has died out as a living

Fig. 56   Etching-aquatint by Goya, from his 'Caprichos'. ¿Donde va Mama? (Where is Mother going?) *The picture relates to the notion of a witch with dropsy being taken for an outing by the best flyers. The umbrella-borne cat is something of a mystery, but is no doubt the ubiquitous familiar*

*Fig. 57   Witch anointing herself with flying salve, with familiar cat and toads.
Illustration used for display in the Museum of Witchcraft at Bayonne, after R. H.
Robbins,* The Encyclopaedia of Witchcraft and Demonology, *1959*

reality or superstition in our present century, and now survives only in the semi-humorous illustrative tradition of fairy tales (figure 19). However, what appears to be a serious report in the *Sunday Chronicle* of 9 September 1928 seemed to resurrect the old notion of witchcraft, for this tells how a woman from Horseheath, near Cambridge, entered into some form of contract with a 'black man', who gave her five 'imps'. These were a rat, a toad, a ferret, a mouse and (of course) a cat.

It is hardly surprising that when a modern artist was commissioned to draw a picture of a young witch for the Witchcraft Museum at Bayonne, in France, he depicted a naked woman greasing her body (presumably with 'flying ointment' in preparation for making the flight to the sabbat), while a black cat rubbed its fur against her feet. He might have had Goya's Caprichos in mind (figure 57), yet his choice of symbols was determined by a tradition far older. This exhibition cat, like the frogs and toads in the foreground to the same picture, are a sign of just how far the cat has been demoted in its symbolism – from a companion of liberty to the demonic attendant of a witch. The modern artist was adopting a feline symbolism well over half a millennium old.

Several of the corbels on the mediaeval exterior of Modena cathedral are carved into the face of different species of cats (figures 58 and 59), and it is possible to interpret these feline heads in much the same way as the demonic gargoyles and other devil-like corbels which are found in great numbers on the façades of most mediaeval church architecture: they are, in other words, representatives of evil.

This supposition is born out by the (later) cat-faced gargoyle on the exterior of the parish church of Littleborough in Lancashire (Plate 25), for the stone figure is in the best tradition of demonology. What make all the Littleborough gargoyles particularly interesting are the occult glyphs which have been carved on the sides of each of them. In the example of figure 25 we see a spiral, one of the occult symbols of the life-force which, when followed in the clockwise direction, carries one into the centre. In some contexts this centre is the Self, in others God. One presumes that since the spiral is found here in a distinctly demonic context, it is to be followed widdershins, which takes one outwards so that one is visualized as dispersing one's energies into the material realm. Interestingly enough, it is the lunar force which is dispersive, and we need hardly point once again to the connexion between cat and Moon.

Cliviger in Lancashire – not far from Littleborough – has its own cat mythology with undertones which may be traced back even further, to Persian tales, themselves perhaps from India. The story, told in

Fig. 58   Cat-head corbels on the fourteenth-century exterior of Modena Cathedral

Joshua Holden's *History of Todmorden*, concerns a beautiful heiress called
Lady Sybil, who lived at Bernshaw Tower. Her favourite walk was to
Eagle Crag, where she would stand and gaze into the wooded chasm
beneath. She began to wish for the power of a witch to fly over the
woods, and eventually bartered her soul in return for the occult powers,
choosing thereafter to roam the hills in the form of a white doe. Lady
Sybil was loved by Lord William of Hapton Tower, but she rejected his
suit and, following the custom of the day, he turned to a local witch
(Mother Helston) in resort to supernatural means to acquire the object of
his love. She advised him to capture the milk-white doe he would see
near Eagle Crag, and take it captive to Hapton Tower. The young man
did this, and in the morning found in place of the doe his beautiful Lady
Sybil, who then conveniently renounced her witchpower and married
Lord William. However, once a witch, always a witch, and the old longing for flight and change came over the woman, so she began to indulge

her power of transformation. One day, as she was playing in the form of a white cat in Cliver Mill, the miller accidentally cut off one of her paws. Lady Sybil returned home with one of her hands missing. Her husband failed to understand her true misery for he questioned her about the costly signet ring which she had worn, and which had vanished with the hand. The tale ends in euphoria, for her magical skill enabled her to restore her hand, and this brought harmony once more into her married life. She no longer transformed herself into a white cat, and seemingly died in peace after a long life. Even so, it is said that on All Hallow's Eve a spectral huntsman pursues a white doe past Eagle Crag.

As I mentioned in the Preface (page 4), there is one quite fascinating moment in the delightful film *Bell, Book and Candle* when the audience is permitted to see the action through the eyes of the cat 'familiar'. During this time the witch views the world through a wide-angle vision. The name of this familiar, Pyewacket, was almost certainly lifted from a crude English woodcut of 1647 (figure 60), which portrayed the infamous self-styled 'Witchfinder General' Matthew Hopkins with two of his unfortunate suspects, who are naming their 'imps' or familiars. The lady to Hopkins' left names her second familiar 'Pyewacket'. In the

Fig. 59   Cat-head corbel on the fourteenth-century exterior of Modena Cathedral

Fig. 60   Frontispiece to Hopkins' Discovery of Witches (1647), showing the so-called
'Witchfinder General', Matthew Hopkins, with two of his witch-victims. Each woman
names her familiars: the lady to the left of Hopkins calls one of her imps 'Pyewackett',
the name adopted for the 'familiar' cat in the film Bell, Book and Candle

actual records of the case, however, the cat was referred to as
Pynewacket. The suspect to the right of Hopkins is Elizabeth Clarke,
pointing to her imp named Holt, who was 'a white kitling'. Both these
ladies were hanged, and their associations with their supposed demonic
imps played a great part in their conviction.

The reason why the courts were so interested in the names of the cats
and other familiars is itself indirectly linked with magic. It was believed
that the cat was merely a disguise for a demon, and if the name of the
demon was known, it would be possible to exorcise it more easily. This
almost certainly explains why the names of so many of these sixteenth-
and seventeenth-century cats have been preserved, and it was certainly
no accident that Shakespeare should have used named cats as witch

familiars in the opening scene to *Macbeth*.

Not all the 'familiar imps' in the witchcraft records are so awful as the Hopkins picture would suggest, and some suspected of harbouring imps did go free. For example, at the Maidstone (Kent) sessions in 1652, six people were found guilty of witchcraft and hanged, but two, who had been charged with employing evil spirits, one in the likeness of a white kitten called Bess, and the other in the likeness of a black kitten called Katt, were found not guilty, and set free. Had the jury believed the two kittens to be imps, the women would have been hanged.

Richard Bovet, the seventeenth-century writer on sorcery, tells how the witches tormented the wife and son of a man named Seavington in the county of Somerset. She would have nightmare visions of a large black cat, which together with seven or nine other felines would make a dreadful yelling for about quarter of an hour, and then vanish. When they had gone, the lady was attacked by fits and internal pains. The two pet cats of the household would fly whenever the demon-cats appeared, and afterwards they starved or pined as though distressed by the demonic invasion.

By the next century, however, the witchcraft craze had diminished to such an extent that the cat was no longer regarded as a potential familiar, and was once again capable of being the subject of poetry. The eighteenth-century poet Christopher Smart wrote a most remarkable poem about his cat Jeoffry, who was imprisoned with his master in the London madhouse, and with the poetic insight of madmen he sees the cat not as demonic but rather as an adversary of the Devil, as 'the servant of the living God':

> For he counteracts the powers of darkness by his
>   electrical skin and glaring eyes.
> For he counteracts the Devil, who is death, by
>   brisking about the life.

Is Christopher Smart writing more about himself than about his cat? When he composed this poem, he was incarcerated in London's Bedlam. The very word lunatic is derived from the Latin for the Moon; and even in Smart's day it was still widely believed that the lunatic's behaviour was subject to the phases of the Moon, as were the eyes of the cat. A print reproduced by Oldfield Howey shows the fool, with a mediaeval head-dress with cat's ears, holding the crescent moon in his hands. This is a striking image which yokes together the four notions of the crescent moon, the demonic horns (themselves said to be symbolic of the lunar crescent), the cat's ears and the 'fool' or insane person who is under the control of the moon. We recall the witch in Shakespeare's *Tempest*, who is:

> A witch; and one so strong
> She could control the moon – make flows and ebbs,

To have control over the moon was tantamount to having control over the demons who dwell within the lunar sphere, as well as having power over the minds of many humans who were themselves so much smitten by the lunar power that they were lunatics.

More immediately dramatic witchcraft records of such cat-magic may be seen in various museums in Britain. For example, in the Moyse's Museum, Bury St Edmunds, is the mummified body of a kitten or puppy (figure 61) which had been strangled at birth and thrust into a chimney as a magical spell against witchcraft. It was once a fairly common practice to brick up a cat or kitten in the wall of a newly constructed house, to provide much the same service against the evil eye. There are examples of such preserved feline cadavers in the museum at Elgin in Scotland.

Some of the most remarkable of all original witchcraft drawings are those attributed to the Reverend Miles Gale, who was the rector at Keighley parish church. The drawings are sometimes said to have been made during the actual trials at York Castle, but this is not possible, as the trials took place in 1622, almost a century before Gale's active life. The drawings (figures 53 and 54), now preserved in the British Library, illustrate a long account of a witchcraft trial compiled by Edward Fairfax of Fewstone, in the Forest of Knaresborough, the text of which was printed in William Gainge's *Daemonologia* of 1882. The details of this complex case need not concern us here, but we should note that three of the six women charged with bewitching the children of Edward Fairfax were said to be attended by cat familiars. Margaret Waite the young, 'impudent and lewd', was aided by a white cat spotted with black, named Inges. Jennet Dibb had been attended 'for forty years by a spirit in the shape of a great black cat, called Gibb'. This featured in one of the Miles Gale drawings, along with a number of other rather fearsome and unexpected diabolical familiars (figure 52). Another unnamed suspect, 'a strange woman', had for twenty years the likeness of a white cat called Fillie (figure 53). Margaret Waite the elder had a familiar which was 'a deformed thing with many feet, the bigness of a cat'.

Fig. 61   Mummified body of a newly-born kitten or puppy, found in an internal chimney of a house – one of the remnants of belief in witchcraft. From the Moyse's House Museum, Bury St Edmunds

The case against the women was that they had bewitched the children into a state where they had strange fits and visions. In the October of 1621, the 16-year-old Helen had 'spectral visions' of Lucifer in numberless forms, a dragon with three heads dripping blood, a handsome suitor in the shape of a prince who suggested suicide, and so on. The visions became a sort of epidemic, and other children were drawn into the condition.

At one stage, Helen appears to have been on speaking terms with one of the voluble cat familiars, as well as with some spirit-birds: she also claimed that she had seen the cats suck the witches' paps. The Assizes were held at York on 1 April 1622, and continued with intervals until the next Assizes, during which time two of the children claimed that they had been blinded by a black cat, presumably acting on the orders of the witches. More visions were indulged in by the children, and on one occasion Helen saw herself being put into the river and carried for miles over hedges and water by a witch and a black cat. When the cats appeared to Helen on another occasion she made them read such verses in the Bible as related directly to familiars.

The suspects were acquitted in August 1622, and it is believed that twelve-year-old Maud Jeffray, one of the afflicted children, confessed to imposture and that the Court had her father gaoled.

It is difficult to make sense of the numerous references to cat-familiars in the English witchcraft trials without recalling again the fact that cats were sacred in the pagan lore which was swept aside by Christianity.

Again, there may have been some racial memory at work, for the ferocious wild cats were by no means extinct in England during the period when the witchcraft craze was at its height.

We have seen how the lunar goddess Freya had two lynxes to draw her celestial carriage, and in this myth there is encapsulated an important historical truth. The cat was domesticated in Egypt in relatively early times, but the cats of northern Europe were wild cats. Indeed, the Freya lynx is often wrongly described as a wild cat. I wonder if this prevalence of wild cats in Europe accounts for the connexion between the cat and black magic in the north. It is unlikely that the first of the Egyptian cats reached even Rome in great numbers until the beginning of our era. (Palladius, writing in 350 AD, mentions the animal as widely distributed in Italy.) The earliest record in the north comes from Austria, where manufactured bricks of the third century show the imprints of a cat's paw accidentally left as it prowled near to what was probably a pottery workshop or kiln. The modern naturalist Guggisberg records that the domestic cat appears to have been quite rare in England even up to the tenth century, though forest wild cats were still common. If, as is widely accepted, many of the practices described in witchcraft literature were mangled offshoots of the ancient religions, we may safely assume that the cat of those pagan times was scarcely the mild-mannered tabby with which we are familiar today. Almost all the cats known to pagan Europeans were probably untamed.

Egyptian laws forbade the export of cats, and elsewhere the weasel was tamed to keep down rats and mice; as a result the cat is usually regarded as feral in classical literature. Ovid tells us that Hecate would sometimes turn herself into a cat, and Apuleius has his witches transform into cats. These were almost certainly wild cats. It follows that when in the Middle Ages the Moon became associated with Purgatory and the cat became symbol of evil because of its link with the Moon goddesses, the savagery of the old wild cats was appropriate to the savagery of the purgatorial demons. Perhaps this notion, itself also derived from the mystery wisdom, accounts for Pope Gregory IX's pronouncement. In early times one of the most popular images for the Devil was a black cat.

The late-classical associations were thus carried on by the thirteenth-century papacy, and formed certain of the accusations laid against the Knights Templars, who certainly worshipped no demons but were themselves involved in the esoteric movement of the time.

The savagery of the untamed cat is often exaggerated, and it has been shown that several species may be easily tamed, yet the forest wild cat, which was once widely distributed throughout Britain and still survives in the Highlands of Scotland can be a very ferocious fighter. The animal photographer Seton Gordon records in his *Days with the Golden Eagle* (1927) a successful fight between a wild cat and an eagle, which died in the encounter. The naturalist Frances Pitt has left an interesting account of an attempt to tame a couple of the creatures which she found in Scotland, and records that the 'pale green eyes glared hatred at human beings'. She christened her next feline experiment, 'a weak scrap of yellow-grey tabby fur', Satan. The larger wild cats such as the lion, tiger and leopard, have horrendous reputations for violence, though they rarely attack humans unprovoked. The 'Leopard of Rudraprayag' is still commemorated in Garhwal, India, by a plaque. It is said to have killed 125 humans before being shot by Corbett in May 1926. Afterwards Corbett measured it the 'honest way', using marker pegs, and found that it was 2.28 metres long. (The 'dishonest way' of measuring was along the curves of the animal, which gave a longer extent, and with what was called the 'Viceroy's measure' – a tape with 11 inches to the foot to make the kill more impressive.) One of the earliest surviving 'cat pictures' is in ivory, the Assyrian panel from Nimrod, probably of the ninth century BC, and now preserved in the British Museum. It shows a lion holding a human by his throat. In the Victoria and Albert Museum is an 'amusing' man-eating tiger, made in the form of an organ. The many tales of tigers or lions occasionally killing humans are only less horrific than the constant history of humans killing tigers and lions.

In the city of Paris it used to be a Midsummer custom to burn in the Place de Grève a basket or sack full of cats. After the conflagration, people would collect the ashes and take them home as magical charms, for they were believed to have a powerful protective virtue. A similar inhuman Midsummer festival was held in Metz, and in the department of the Ardennes on the first Sunday in Lent, in Alsace at Easter. These practices were undeniably derived from pagan rites: there is adequate evidence to show that the Druids (or, at least, the degenerate priestcraft derived from the Druidic cult) would enclose live animals in wickerwork baskets for roasting to death – yet they were popularized and rationalized in the Christian communities by the belief that the Devil, or his slaves the witches, might appear in the form of the cat. Thus are the Egyptians and Roman gods debased.

When Sir James Frazer asked the question why humans and animals (especially the cat) should be killed in such a cruel way, he came to the conclusion that the rites were connected with attempts to break the power of witchcraft: 'All these victims, we may surmise, were doomed to the flames, not because they were animals, but because they were believed to be witches who had taken the shape of animals for their nefarious purposes.'

The romantic haze which colours the modern view of cats often prevents us from understanding some of the meaning in feline symbols used by artists in the past. For example, Erwin Panofsky interprets the four animals gathered around Adam and Eve in Dürer's 1504 engraving (figure 62) as representing the four temperaments – the elk as the earthly melancholia, the cat as choleric cruelty, the rabbit as sanguine sensuality and the ox as the sluggish phlegmatic. But there are other ways of interpreting the symbolism of the cat in the early sixteenth century. The cat in Dürer's engraving is contemplating the mouse to the left, and Panofsky suggests that this little feline drama, of the cat ready to spring upon the mouse, represents the feline predatory nature of the woman Eve, while the mouse represents the weak and susceptible nature of man. In fact, this symbolism is quite inappropriate, for it could just as well be reversed, making Eve weak and susceptible and Adam predatory. There is a much more sensible way of looking at this confrontation, within the

Fig. 62   Detail of cat, from figure 34. From the Dürer etching 'Adam and Eve', 1504

framework of the fifteenth-century view of the cat, which is to see the feline as a representative of evil. This would explain why it has its tail curled around the foot of Eve, for it is like the Devil-serpent curled around the tree, passing the fruit into Eve's hand with its mouth. The tail of the mouse is clearly pointing to Adam's foot just as insistently as the cat's tail is wrapped around Eve: in this way the mouse symbolizes what is being 'lost' to the cat, which is of course Mankind. Thus, if the cat represents the Devil, then the mouse represents the Fall. This view that the cat symbolizes the demonic element would explain its important placing at the foot of the tree, where it seems to perform the function of separating Adam and Eve on the earth. Then, if we were to 'reject' the cat as one of the four symbols of the elements, we could make sense of the presence of the parrot above Adam's head. A bird appears in several mediaeval images as representative of the temperament of sanguinity, and is a far more appropriate symbol of air than is the rabbit, whose sexual life makes it a more fitting symbol for the choleric.

The truth is that the mediaeval world saw the cat in a darker light than we do in modern times. For example, when the Florentine Christopher de Honesti wrote a treatise on poisons and antidotes, and concerned himself with the bite of the cat, he was convinced that the bite was sufficiently poisonous to turn the whole body green, and he accepted the well-established tradition that the brain of the cat was a poison when eaten. One of the unseemly 'experiments' involving a cat in the *Liber vaccae* recorded by Lynn Thorndike in her *History of Magic and Experimental Science*, indicates something of the late mediaeval attitude to cats – though, of course, the magical spell is probably merely a copy of a much older version. The aim of this spell is to enable the magician to see spirits. A white cock is fed for three successive days on the eyes of three fish of a particular kind (the eyes having been removed while the fish were still living), and on the third hour of the third day the cock is decapitated and fed to a wild cat, which is in turn beheaded. It is from the body of this unfortunate cat that the blood and gall are taken, dried and used to make a concoction which will enable one to see spirits. The role of the cat, albeit a wild cat, in demonological texts indicates something of the nature of the Satanic beliefs with which Dürer would be familiar, at a time when the German witchcraft craze was in full swing.

Conclusion

THE MAGIC OF NINE

The 9 is the mystic number of great power . . . it is strong, unswerving, protective and creative, and is harmoniously related to the spiritual world. This harmony is reflected in its form, for the enclose in the upper half is linked with the space of Heaven, and the open form in the lower half is linked with the Earth . . . This idea of incarnating from the upper spiritual to the lower material (from the circle to the curve below) is expressed in the adage of the numerologists that '9 is the alpha and omega of human possibilities, the beginning and the end.'

F. GETTINGS, *Encyclopedia of the Occult*

Popular superstition grants the cat nine lives, yet, as we have seen, the feline has a hundred different disguises and a hundred different names. However, most superstitions are merely debased spiritual truths, unconscious memories of esoteric wisdom, and we must ask why the number nine is so persistent in relation to the cat?

It would seem that the number, like so many other beliefs about the cat, goes back to the Egyptian mystery lore. The number nine has always been regarded as sacred, because it is three times three, the Trinity repeated three times, and the ancient world also had its trinities. In the ancient world of Heliopolis, the nine gods were Atmu, Shu, Tefnu, Geb, Nut, Osiris, Isis, Set and Nepthys, each of which was linked in some way with the cat. It could be this ennead of gods and goddesses which encouraged the early writers of the Church to determine that there were nine ranks of angelic beings. Each was linked with a planetary or stellar function, stretching from the Angels of the Moon, through the Exsusiai of the Sun, up to the Thrones of Saturn (where time itself ends), then out into the eternal realm of the Seraphim and Cherubim who had rule over the stars and the zodiac.

A sacred cat amulet and certain cat figurines which have survived illustrate this numerology of three or nine. A blue-glazed amulet representing a cat and kittens, dated circa 600 BC and now in the British Museum, shows six kittens beneath the protective arms of the mother cat and two sitting on her arms – these, with the mother herself, make a total of nine cats.

The sistrum, which accompanied as primitive music the ancient rituals, and which is in the hands of the ancient goddess Bast in figure 11, is also involved in the numerology of nine within a feline context. The sistrum had a variety of forms, but the most common had a cat's head (sometimes with a human face) on the upper bend of the instrument. Within the inner space were four little bars, each representing one of the four elements: it is said that the agitation of these bars represented the motion of the four elements within the material realm, by means of which form arises and is destroyed. On either side of the instrument were the faces of the goddesses Nepthys and Isis, representing death and life, respectively. The sistrum itself therefore combined nine symbolic elements – the handle by which it was shaken to make music, the containing form (itself reminiscent of the Ru symbol) of the instrument, the four bars, the heads of the two goddesses and the cat's head. The sistrum was passed on into the mystery wisdom of Rome, for paintings found at Portici show a priest of Isis and a kneeling woman shaking the instrument. Oldfield Howey notes that a similar instrument was used by the singing girls of Japan. Not so very long ago the Tokyo geisha girls subscribed to a Mass for the souls of those cats whose lives had been sacrificed in order to provide the material which was an integral part of these instruments.

The mediaeval Church demoted the cat as part of the official programme of 'spiritual reform'. The ancient mystery wisdom, which the Church had failed to fully understand, was to be demystified, and the ancient gods turned into demons. The cat, which had been among the most sacred of all animals, was to suffer the most. The cat had found no mention in the Bible, and, since it was not protected by holy writ, it became an easy prey for the churchmen in search of a demonic scapegoat. The Gnostic text which we now call the *Pistis Sophia*, and which was probably as old as the Gospels, described great cats in the halls of punishment:

> Jesus tells the Virgin Mary: the outer darkness is a great serpent, the tail of which is in its mouth, and it is outside the whole world, and surroundeth the whole world; in it there are many places of punishment, and it containeth twelve halls wherein severe punishment is inflicted . . . The governor of the second hall hath as his true face the face of a cat, and they call him in his place Kharakhar . . . And in the eleventh hall there are many governors, and there are seven heads, each of them having as its true face the face of a cat; and the greatest of them, who is over them, they call in his place Rokhar.

This text (for all its wisdom and Christianity) was eventually dismissed as heretical, but could it be that such 'forbidden' literature furnished the later Church with a rationale for visualizing the cat in demonic form? Within centuries the cat had been turned into a Devil, and still later into the witch's familiar. How far removed from the goddess is the fat cat among the misericords of Malvern Priory which is being hanged by three rats.

Yet, in spite of the Church, the company of nine gods and goddesses lingered in a misunderstood form in the popular mind, in the notion that the cat somehow had nine lives. As the power of the Church waned, the cat began to creep back into sanctity. By the end of the eighteenth century when, as we have seen, the astronomer Lalande redisposed the stars into different constellations, he felt himself free enough to make one of them a cat (Plate 13). Unconsciously he was returning the creature to its rightful place as a celestial goddess. Was the constellation of *Felis* not adopted into the later star-maps of the astronomers because the world is not yet ready to recognize the truth, for so long hidden by mediaeval self-interest, that the cat is indeed a creature of the gods, a symbol of light and life rather than of darkness and death?

In modern times the cat has been stripped of most of its ancient symbolism and is universally reduced to a role of decorator, appearing in a myriad of greetings cards and advertisements, where the notions of slyness, sensuousness, softness or smoothness are required or where an inimitable aloofness of style, mingling with an evocation of the traditional 'good luck' associated with the black cat of popular lore, is needed to paint a mood or to hide a subliminal message of more or less superficial significance. A modern exception to this general trend is the use of feline symbolism in the Kuykendall tarot series and is found, perhaps surprisingly, in a few drawings by Paul Klee and Picasso, as in the work of a few lesser known yet equally dedicated artists such as the Jewish artist Fay Pomerance, who (without in the least straining ancient mythologies) links the feline nature with the demon-consort of the first man, Adam, in her treatment of the Lilith theme (Plate 26). Her cat with nine tails (the 'cat o' nine tails', perhaps, which nowadays flagellates the progeny of Adam?) is a materialized version of the popular cat with nine lives, yet is still linked with the dark part of mankind which, according to Talmudic legend, gave rise to the brood of demons. This feline Lilith is all too aware that the Fall of Man is now proceeding apace, and, unlike the sleepy cat of Dürer's print (figure 62), she has already gripped the mouse-victim (Man himself) by the tail. Is the fish, secure in the other feline hind paw, symbol of the redemptive power of the battered Christ, the light which alone may counter the darkness within?

Bibliography

ACKERMANN, A. S. E., *Popular Fallacies*, London, 1950 edition.

ADAMS, George, *Physical and Ethereal Spaces*, London, 1965.

AYMES, C. A. W., *The Pictorial Language of Hieronymus Bosch*, translated from the German by E. A. Frommer, Horsham, 1975.

BARDENS, Dennis, *Psychic Animals: an Investigation of their Secret Powers*, London, 1987.

BAX, D., *Hieronymus Bosch his picture-writing decyphered*, Amsterdam, 1979.

BEADLE, M., *The Cat. History, Biology and Behaviour*, London, 1977.

BEAUMONT, F., & FLETCHER, J., *Bonduca*, London, 1614.

BEATTY, Clyde, *Facing the Big Cats* (Clyde Beatty and Edward Anthony), London, 1965.

BLAVATSKY, H. P., *The Secret Doctrine*, London, 1888.

BOGUET, Henri, *Discours de Sourciers*, translated as *An Examen of Witches* (see also the translation by E. A. Ashwin, Bungay), 1929.

BOVET, Richard, *Pandaemonium*, London, 1684.

BOYLE, Robert *See* THORNDIKE.

BOZZANO, Ernest, *Les Manifestations Metapsychiques et les Animaux*, Paris, 1926.

BRAU, Jean-Louis, *Larousse Encyclopedia of Astrology* (J.-L. Brau, Helen Weaver and Allan Edmands), New York, 1977.

BRERETON *See* PERRAULT.

BREWER, E.C., *Brewer's Dictionary of Phrase and Fable*, London, 1963 edition.

BRIGGS, K., *Folktales of England* (edited by Katharine M. Briggs and Ruth L. Tongue), Chicago, 1965.

BRODEUR *See* STURLUSON.

BROOKE, H. C., *Cat Gossip* (edited by H. C. Brooke), Taunton, 1926, etc.

BUDGE, E. A. Wallis, *Book of the Dead* (Papyrus of Hunefer, Anhai, Kerasher and Netchemet), London, 1899.

BUDGE, E. A. Wallis, *The Gods of the Egyptians*, London, 1904.

BUDGE, E. A. Wallis, *The Book of the Dead* (translated from the Egyptian hieroglyphic by Budge), London, 1923.

BURTON, Maurice, *The Sixth Sense of Animals*, London, 1973.

CAMPBELL, John Gregorson, *Witchcraft*

and Second Sight in the Highlands and Islands of Scotland, Glasgow, 1902 (reprinted Wakefield, Yorkshire, 1974).

CRUIKSHANK, George, Fairy Library, London, 1870.

DALE-GREEN, Patricia, Cult of the Cat, London, 1963 (reprinted Boston, 1963, with title The Archetypal Cat).

DANCE, Peter, Animal Fakes and Frauds, Maidenhead, 1976.

DAVIS, Andrew Jackson, The Diakka, and their Earthly Victims, New York, 1873.

DAVIS, F. Hadland, Myths and Legends of Japan, London, 1920.

DENT, Anthony, Lost Beasts of Britain, London, 1974.

DINET, Des Hieroglyphiques, 1607.

DORLING, E. E., Leopards of England, London, 1913.

EDDA See STURLUSON.

ELIOT, Thomas Stearns, Old Possum's Book of Practical Cats, London, 1939.

ELIOT, Thomas Stearns, Four Quartets, New York, 1943.

ERASTUS, T. See THORNDIKE.

EVANS, E. P., Animal Symbolism in Ecclesiastical Architecture, London, 1896.

EVANS, Joan, Magical Jewels in the Middle Ages and the Renaissance, 1976.

EWEN, C. L'Estrange, Witch Hunting and Witch Trials, London, 1929 (reprinted London, 1974).

EWEN, C. L'Estrange, Witchcraft and Demonianism, London, 1933 (reprinted London, 1970).

FAIRFAX, Edward, Daemonologia (manuscript Add 32496 in British Library, but printed by W. Gainge in 1882).

FLUDD, Robert See THORNDIKE.

FRASER, J. G., The Golden Bough, London, 1933.

FRIEDMANN, H., A Bestiary for St

Jerome. Animal symbolism in European Religious Art, Washington, 1980.

FULCANELLI, Fulcanelli: Master Alchemist. Le Mystère des Cathédrales, London, 1971.

GAINGE, William, Daemonologia, 1882.

GALLICO Paul, The Silent Miaow. Translated from the Feline by Paul Gallico. Photographs by Jane Burton. London and Sydney, 1964.

GARDNER, Martin, The Annotated Alice, London, 1970.

GEBELIN, Court de, Le Monde Primitif, Paris, 1781.

GESNER, C., Historia Animalium, 1551.

GIFFORD, George, Discourse of the Subtle Practise of Devils by Witches and Sorcerers, 1587.

GREENE, David, Incredible Cats. The Secret Powers of Your Pet, London, 1984.

GUBERNATIS, Angelo de, Zoological Mythology, London, 1872.

GUERBER, H. A., Myths of the Norsemen, London, 1909.

GUGGISBERG, C. A. W., Wild Cats of the World, London, 1975.

HAMPSO, Paule V., The Cat-Lover's Journal.

HENRY, William, The Scottish Tartans, with the Badges, Arms, Slogans, etc. of the Clans.

HOWEY, Oldfield M., The Cat in the Mysteries of Religion and Magic, 1923.

JEFFREY, Percy, Whitby Lore and Legend, 1923.

JONSON, Benjamin, Masque of Queens, c. 1609.

KLINGENDER, Francis, Animals in art and thought to the end of the Middle Ages, London, 1971.

KUYKENDALL, Karen, Tarot of the Cat People, New York, 1985.

LALANDE, J. J. le Francais de, Bibliographie Astronomique, Paris, 1805.

LAMBSPRINCK, De Lapide Philosophico, Frankfurt, 1677.

LANGTON, N. and B., *The Cat in Ancient Egypt*, Cambridge, 1940.

LELAND, C., *Aradia, or the Gospel of the Witches*, London, 1887.

LEWIS, C. S., *The Last Battle*, 1956. The edition with the Pauline Baynes illustrations was published under the Collins Fontana imprint, 1980.

MCLEAN, Adam, *The Triple Goddess*, Edinburgh, 1983.

MACLEOD, N., *Reminiscences of a Highland Parish*, 1867 (new edition London, 1910).

MANNING, Olivia, *Extraordinary Cats*, London, 1967.

MASSEY, Gerald, *The Natural Genesis*, London, 1883.

MATHER, Cotton, *The Wonders of the Invisible World*, London, 1693.

MEGNIN, P., *Notre Ami Le Chat*, 1899.

MELLEN, I. M., *The Science and Mystery of the Cat*, New York, 1940.

MERY, Ferdinand, *The Life, History and Magic of the Cat*, London, 1967.

MURRAY, Margaret, *The Witch Cult in Western Europe*, Oxford, 1921.

NECKER, C., *Four Centuries of Cat Books*, New York, 1972.

NECKHAM, Alexander, *De Naturis Rerum See* the T. Wright version in *Rerum Britannicarum Medii Aevi Scriptores*, London, 1863.

O'DONNELL, Elliott, *Animal Ghosts*, London, 1913.

OUSPENSKY, P. D., *In Search of the Miraculous*, London, 1947.

PANOFSKY, Erwin, *Albrecht Dürer*, London, 1948.

PERRAULT, C., *Fairy Tales* (translation by G. Brereton), London, 1921.

PETRIE, W. M. Flinders, *Amulets*, London, 1914.

PETTO, S., *A Faithful Narrative*, London, 1652.

PITCAIRN, Robert, *Criminal Trials*, Edinburgh, 1833.

PLANCY, Collin de, *Dictionnaire Infernal*, 1863 edition.

PLUTARCH, *Isis and Osiris*.

PUCKELD, *Folk Beliefs of the Southern Negro*.

ROBBINS, R. Hope, *The Encyclopaedia of Witchcraft and Demonology*, London, 1959.

ROWLAND, Beryl, *Animals with Human Faces*, London, 1974.

SCHOTT, Gaspard, *Magiae Universalis*, Leiden, 1657.

SCOT, Reginald, *The Discoverie of Witchcraft*, London, 1584.

SHARPE, C. K., *A Historical Account of the Belief in Witchcraft in Scotland*, London, 1884.

STRAPAROLA, Giovanni, *Piacevoli Notti*, Bari, 1927 (reprinted Rome–Bari, 1975).

STURLUSON, Snorri, *Prose Edda* (translated by A. C. Brodeur), New York, 1929.

SULLIVAN, Edward, *The Book of Kells*, London, Paris, New York, 1915.

SUMMERS, M., *The History of Witchcraft and Demonology*, London, 1926.

THORNDIKE, Lynn, *History of Magic and Experimental Science*, New York, 1941.

TOPSELL, E., *The Historie of Foure-Footed Beastes*, London, 1607.

TRUNGPA, Chogyam, *Cutting Through Spiritual Materialism*, edited by John Baker and Marvin Casper, Watkins, 1973.

WATERTON *See* DANCE.

WOOD, J. G., *The Illustrated Natural History*, London, 1897.

YOGANANDA, Paramhansa, *Autobiography of a Yogi*, 1969 edition.

YORK, 'Depositions of York Castle'. Quoted in *Surtees Society*, Vol. 40, p. 67.

INDEX

Index

Numbers in italic refer to captions